A Very Short,
Fairly Interesting and
Reasonably Cheap
Book About
International Business

A Very Short, Fairly Interesting and Reasonably Cheap Book About International Business

George Cairns and Martyna Śliwa

Los Angeles • London • New Delhi • Singapore • Washington DC

HD
62.4
C 136

First published 2008

SAGE Publications Ltd
1 Oliver's Yard
55 City Road
London EC1Y 1SP

SAGE Publications Inc.
2455 Teller Road
Thousand Oaks, California 91320

SAGE Publications India Pvt Ltd
B 1/I 1 Mohan Cooperative Industrial Area
Mathura Road
New Delhi 110 044

SAGE Publications Asia-Pacific Pte Ltd
33 Pekin Street #02-01
Far East Square
Singapore 048763

Library of Congress Control Number: 2008922733

British Library Cataloguing in Publication data

A catalogue record for this book is available from
the British Library

ISBN 978-1-4129-4762-6
ISBN 978-1-4129-4763-3 (pbk)

Typeset by C&M Digitals (P) Ltd, Chennai, India
Printed in Great Britain by Athenaeum Press, Gateshead
Printed on paper from sustainable resources

Contents

Contents

Acknowledgements

This book is born of a relatively short collaboration between two academics of different generations, gender, nationality and disciplinary background. Brought together by chance, we discovered a common desire to bring consideration of some of the critical issues that impact everybody to the fore in discussion of international business (IB) in literature addressed at students of management and related areas. The invitation from Sage to write a book for this series offered an opportunity that we could not miss, to present our view of international business from its historical origins to its broad ranging interconnections with society, politics, economy and environment in the present. In developing our own standpoint and our knowledge, we have been inspired and assisted by a number of people, whose input we would like to acknowledge here.

First, we owe a great debt of gratitude to Steffen Böhm (Essex University) who has given us feedback on parts of the text as it developed, has offered us insights into some of the alternative forms of IB that we present, and has challenged our perceptions of ourselves as involved actors in IB activities on a range of levels. We have also received feedback on parts of the text and suggestions for refinement from Joanne Roberts (Newcastle University). Prem Sikka (Essex University) has supplied information and sources on issues of taxation, tax avoidance and accounting. Jerry Coakley (Essex University), Neil Kellard (Essex University) and Chris Land (Essex University) have also commented on sections of the book and have always been prepared to engage in conversations about it. Our involvement in the journal *Critical Perspectives on International Business* has provided us with links to a number of writers in the field whose work has inspired us, including Bobby Banerjee (Western Sydney University), Grazia Ietto-Gillies (London South Bank University) and Martin Parker (Leicester University). We must also acknowledge the inspiration for our analytic framework offered by the work of Bent Flyvbjerg (Aalborg

University). In addition, we would like to thank the anonymous reviewers, whom Sage invited to comment on our original proposal, for their strong encouragement and constructive critique.

Finally, we are grateful to our friends and families for the numerous conversations from which we have drawn ideas for this book and for all the support they have given us over the time of working on it. In particular, we would like to thank Angela Irvine, Anna and Michał Śliwa, and Stephen Betros. Whilst all these people have contributed to the process of shaping this book, we must take personal responsibility for what you now read, particularly any errors that we have allowed to creep in.

George Cairns and Martyna Śliwa
Colchester, 2008

Introduction: Why We Feel the Need to Write This Particular Book on International Business

It is the way that we behave in our dealings with other people that makes us just or unjust.

Aristotle

You are probably wondering what makes this short book on international business (IB) any different from other IB texts that you could have picked up. This is a question that we, as authors, have been asking ourselves since we accepted the publisher's invitation to take on this project. Undoubtedly, as can be inferred from the title, this small volume contains fewer words than the average IB textbook – and is also cheaper. But, is there really anything about it that makes it deserve the accolade of being 'fairly interesting'? We hope so. Let us briefly say why.

First, we trust that you, our reader, will find interesting the way in which our writing has been influenced by how we think about you. Looking at mainstream IB textbooks, it seems to us that they conceptualize the reader as a student of IB, to whom they convey knowledge about 'how to' become a successful manager in international business. Here, success for the individual is dependent upon success for the IB firm, which is by and large measured in terms of making profits for the company and providing a financial return to shareholders. Our key aim in writing this book is to address you not just as a student of, or a (aspiring) manager in, IB – albeit, you may well be so – but as a concerned 'stakeholder' (Freeman, 1984), a 'citizen of the world', who is involved in, affects and is affected by IB practices, and who is implicated in their impacts upon and outcomes for all stakeholders – including future generations.

Second, we hope that you will find interest in our overview of how the current model of IB practice has emerged over time, what ideas and thinking have underpinned its development, and how theories have been constructed in order to explain this. Within most IB textbooks, history and theory (where they are introduced) are, to our minds, used mainly in order to justify and support the dominant paradigm of IB, with its emphasis on the profitability of capitalist enterprise, and market growth and expansion through internationalization and globalization. Whilst they may touch upon critical issues such as 'slave labour', environmental degradation and resource depletion, they see these largely as problems for the firm to overcome in pursuit of the unquestioned aims of growth and profitability. In this book, we draw upon history and theory not just to present how things were and are, but also to convey the idea that the trajectory along which IB has developed has not necessarily been a 'natural', 'inevitable' or the only possible route. In doing this, we draw your attention to the major impact that powerful stakeholders in IB – such as nation states, multinational enterprises (MNEs), and supranational institutions – have had, over time, on developing particular types of IB practice and on the spread of theories that legitimize them.

Finally, our thinking about the implications of IB for all stakeholders and our de-naturalizing of the notion of IB as a value-free process of growth and development leads us to raise topics and issues of concern to us, and to consider aspects of IB other than the strategies for success of the ubiquitous Coca-Cola, McDonald's, Microsoft and the like. As you read on, you will find that we discuss such aspects of IB as the working conditions of those who labour in the fields and in 'sweatshops' – both in 'less developed countries' (LDCs) and in the backstreets of major cities of the 'developed' world – to produce the foodstuffs, clothing, consumer electronics and other products that pervade supermarkets and shopping malls. In addition, we raise issues such as trade in toxic waste disposal, ship breaking in LDCs, and the ethics of staff training in the call centres of India.

Who, then, do we see as the readership of this book? First, we hope that it will appeal to students of management-related subjects who are looking for a short text that provides an overview of relevant theories and practices of IB. Second, we target IB managers who want to understand the theoretical foundations of what they do and why certain strategies are proposed for internationalization of the firm. For both of these groups, as we have outlined above, we hope to move thinking beyond simple 'how to' questions, and to some reflection on issues of 'why' and 'with what effect'. Additionally, we would like to think that our colleagues in the academic community will find this book useful in their pedagogic practice. We hope that it will be of interest to a wider audience, recognizing that we all, whether as employees, consumers or citizens, impact and are impacted by contemporary IB activities, and have the potential to influence their future development. At the same time, we realize that, whilst intended as a 'reasonably cheap' text, this book will not be affordable to potential readers in many countries where the general level of income makes it very expensive. Also, bearing in mind that its distribution will be set within the confines of the publisher's marketing strategy and that it is written in English by western academics, it will remain inaccessible for the majority of the world population. Finally, in writing this short book about international business, we acknowledge that this in itself constitutes an IB project, using resources to generate profit from sales in those markets where demand can be identified.

We trust that, in raising issues of how everyone contributes to the development of and the problems stemming from IB, we can make you aware of these and stimulate your thinking on how you might, through your own actions, make a difference now for the benefit of future generations.

how to read this book

In writing this short text, we assume that you, our readers, are most likely new to studying the field of international business. As such, we seek to write in a simple and accessible way. However, this does not mean that our discussion and arguments are intended as simplistic. Rather, we credit you with intelligence and a critical mind and we assume that you wish to grapple with the complexities and ambiguities of contemporary IB practices, and to consider both why these are as they are and how they might be different. In order to assist this process, we offer a theoretical basis for reflection on these practices from a range of perspectives. In addition, we present a history of IB and its grounding in international trade over the centuries. In doing this, we show that contemporary theories and practices are not value-free and politically neutral, but are grounded in particular European, and later Anglo-American ways of thinking and acting. In addition, we recognize that in your daily life you both affect and are affected by IB practices. As such, we aim to enable you to base your reflection on IB on your own experience and involvement, as well as on the examples that we provide.

Since this is a 'very short' book, we cannot cover every aspect of IB in detail. However, we are aware of the dangers of stereotyping and generalizing inherent in any attempt to provide both a short and a comprehensive account of a discipline. We also acknowledge that we have been selective in including and excluding material, and that other authors could have made different choices and would approach the subject from a different standpoint. For example, where we write about the history of IB theory and practice, out of necessity we present a sequence of conceptual developments and empirical examples. This does not, however, mean that we see history as unfolding in a linear and progressive fashion. We note, for example, that there have been, over the centuries, certain shifts in thinking about who the main actors in international transactions are, and how changes in technologies have impacted IB practice. However, we do not necessarily consider that these have constituted development and contributed to an improvement of the situation of many of those affected. In order to enable you to read beyond our text and to fill in gaps in theory and thinking, we refer you to other sources for more background and more detail. The texts that we point you to represent examples of mainstream IB textbooks, more critical writing on the nature and impact of IB, and more general theoretical works that will hopefully enable you to place your own thinking on IB into a broader context.

At this point, we would emphasize that speaking about IB is only possible on the basis of acceptance of a number of assumptions. For example, that it is natural and beneficial for human beings to engage in economic activity; that the term 'business' corresponds with the actions that people pursue when they undertake this economic activity; that the rules according to which business takes place are to a large extent determined by nation states, and therefore, there is something unique about 'international business'; that, contemporarily, the pursuit of IB is by and large linked to the spread and dominance of capitalism; and that, as a domain of theory and practice, IB is worthy of attention by affected stakeholders, including researchers, educators and students.

In order to clarify our own approach, we outline a few key terms that we use throughout our text and the broad meaning that we attach to each, acknowledging their grounding in the above assumptions:

- *International business* (IB): We read IB as referring to any form of commercial exchange of materials, goods, services or any other resources that involves transfer across national boundaries.
- *Internationalization*: In referring to the internationalization of business and of organizations, we point to their expansion beyond their home nation through establishing relationships, transaction linkages, or operations in one or more other countries.
- *Globalization*: The term globalization is subject to many interpretations and has no single agreed meaning. For some, it represents a natural, inevitable and largely unproblematic move towards a 'borderless world' and the end of the independent nation state. Here, we align with those who read it as the spread of western social, economic and cultural values. Intertwined with this process, we see the imperative of MNEs to configure and develop their value chains at a global level in the aim of making the most of their own efficiency and effectiveness in order to maximize their shareholder value.
- *Neo-liberalism* and the '*Washington Consensus*': The process of globalization that we describe above is underpinned by the advancement

of neo-liberal policies. These support the transfer of control over country economies from the public to the private sector, with privatization of state-owned enterprises (SOEs), development of a free market largely devoid of government intervention, and the elimination of restrictions on firms' decision making. The spread of neo-liberalism is advocated, and in cases enforced, by the 'Washington Consensus' of Washington-based institutions that include not just the US Treasury but also the World Bank and the International Monetary Fund (IMF).

drawing inspiration from Aristotle

As we have outlined above, our approach to IB is based upon consideration of all stakeholders. The 'stakeholder approach' was first articulated by Ed Freeman in 1984 and it has since been applied in discussions of business ethics and how organizations are responsible not only to their financial investors but also to other parties, including society at large. However, thinking about the broad consequences of actions for the whole of humanity has a long history. It can be traced back to the Greek philosophers, in particular, to Aristotle (350BC/2004) and his writings in *The Nicomachean Ethics*. In this work, Aristotle outlines the intellectual virtue of *phronēsis*, generally translated into English as 'practical wisdom' or 'prudence'. Aristotle considers *phronēsis* as a character trait necessary for 'man [sic] to be able to deliberate about what is good and advantageous', and to be 'capable of action with regard to things that are good or bad for man' (Aristotle, 2004: 150) in general. *Phronēsis* implies concern for the good of humanity at large, including present and future generations. As such, this concept has served contemporary writers (e.g. Cairns and Śliwa, 2008; Dunne, 1993; Jentoft, 2006) who address problems of ethics, governance and the impact of the actions of groups and individuals on others. In social science literature, Flyvbjerg (2001: 60) offers a way of approaching inquiry into social phenomena in accordance with *phronēsis* by first asking four seemingly simple questions:

- Where are we going?
- Is this development desirable?

• What, if anything, should we do about it?
• Who gains and who loses, and by which mechanisms of power?

In writing this book, we bear in mind these four questions in relation to various aspects of the theory and practice of IB. As such, we draw upon *phronēsis* to generate discussion from the perspective of a broad range of stakeholders, and to support an understanding of IB theories and activities in terms of their origins, emergence, outcomes and implications.

stakeholders in international business

In the following three chapters of this book, we explain how the theories of international business that have developed over time have placed the benefit of, first, the nation state and then, more recently, the firm, as the key concern of IB. Here, as we have outlined, we attach importance not only to countries and companies, but also to those who are often seen as either marginal to IB practice, or as factors to be 'managed' for the benefit of commercial organizations. Moving beyond the country- or firm-centred approaches, we question the frequently taken-for-granted notion that the underpinning purpose of capitalist organizations is to maximize profits and return on investment for financial stakeholders. The proponents of this assumption often quote the renowned economist Milton Friedman (1962: 133), who stated that:

> There is one and only one social responsibility of business – to use its resources and engage in activities designed to increase its profits so long as it stays within the rules of the game, which is to say, engages in open and free competition, without deception or fraud ... for corporate officials to make as much money for their stockholders as possible.

What is often missed out of the discussion, however, are topics that Friedman himself raised as a counterpoint to the profit motive of private enterprise, namely the duty of the state to attend to matters of health, education and defence, and the question of who looks after the interests of the worker, the consumer and broader society. Below, we briefly discuss some of the impacts of IB on these three categories of stakeholders, and we reflect upon what we identify as problematic issues that ought to be addressed in the context of Flyvbjerg's framework of four questions for developing an analysis in accordance with *phronēsis*.

the worker and international business

When addressing the internal organizational stakeholders, a lot of the IB literature focuses on issues relating to the employment of high-level managers, typically from the countries of the MNE's headquarters, and on how they can perform most effectively for the organization during their term managing overseas operations. However, in thinking about the relationship between the employee and the international business organization, we believe it is important to look at the effects of MNEs on all types and levels of employees – both their own and those of their supplier and client organizations – at a global level. In so doing, we draw attention to issues of socio-economic inequality and poverty, and of exploitation associated with internationalization and globalization of business.

Nowadays, it is common practice for MNEs to configure their 'value chain' internationally or even globally, seeking to gain 'competitive advantage' (Porter, 1985) over their competitors through minimizing their production costs. In so-called 'developed economies', the cost of labour has long been recognized as the major contributor to overall costs of production. This has led firms to shift their production activities to locations that offer lower labour costs, both in terms of wages paid and of provision of infrastructure and employee benefits. The existence of such locations, which are the result of structural discrepancies across countries and regions, underpins the possibilities for attaining competitive advantage through exploitation of global cost differentials. Companies that have moved some or all aspects of their product or service delivery to countries with low costs of employment have a vested interest in maintaining these differentials, whilst 'developing economies' that aspire to gain a foothold on the ladder of economic growth are prepared to market themselves as providers of cheap labour, low or no-cost factories, and tax-free investment opportunities. For both the MNEs that seek out such locations and those countries that offer such opportunities, the impact that these may have on local populations is not seen as problematic.

Critical commentators (e.g. Bauman, 1998; Klein, 2000; Milanovic, 2005; Rapley, 2004) draw attention to the growing inequalities between and within societies as a result of globalization and the development of new models of supply that take advantage of economic differences – for example, using 'sweat shop' labour in one country in order to produce branded goods that generate high levels of profit when sold in another. As Naomi Klein (2000) points out, this fragmentation of global production results in social exclusion and impoverishment for many, with a simultaneous formation of global elites, including those who, thanks to the activities of MNEs, have become the social and economic 'winners' of globalization. As developing countries compete to attract MNEs' production of goods and services, these developments can lead to a 'race to the bottom', exemplified by the continuous deterioration in wage levels in some industries. The acclaimed intellectual Zygmunt Bauman (1998: 72) has stated that, in this age of globalized production and consumption, 'the new rich do not need the poor any more'. But, as you will find as you read on, we consider that the rich need the poor as much as ever. It is just that, where the rich factory owner of the past lived side by side with his workers in the new metropolis of the industrial revolution, the super-rich are now globally mobile and can live in London or Lagos whilst they generate income in Boston or Beijing. In any of these settings, they can remain detached from the workers on whom they rely for wealth generation. The gap between the wealth and mobility of the world's rich and that of the poor takes us to a consideration of another group affected by IB activity, consumers.

▓▓▓▓▓▓ the consumer and international business

Whilst shareholders are the focus of profit distribution for MNEs, consumers are the main focus of how these profits are generated. In this way, individuals external to commercial organizations are mainly conceptualized as actual and potential consumers, rather than as members of society. As such, the central topic of IB texts in relation to consumers is that of marketing strategies and practices to be employed internationally in order to identify them and to target companies' products and services at them. Whilst subjects such as 'market segmentation' are presented as ways of identifying and addressing the needs of consumers, along with differences in culture, taste, purchasing power, etc. between groups in society, socio-economic differences between groups are not viewed as problematic. Rather, they are seen as 'issues' to be addressed by marketers for the benefit of the company, through identifying new market opportunities for existing offerings, or as sources of inspiration for new ones. The demographic characteristics of potential consumers – such as age, gender, race and income – are analyzed in order to find out which sections of society have sufficient purchasing power to fall, potentially, within the marketing radar of the firm. At the same time, any issues of social conflict and injustice, associated with the very 'demographics' of the population, are either ignored or are discussed in the context of their implications for the company's ability to market its products successfully.

Whilst critics of the consumer discourse contend that by referring to people as 'consumers' companies disregard other social roles of individuals, its proponents argue that through concentrating on the needs of the consumer, firms not only meet these needs, but provide the major engine of economic growth and development that will ultimately benefit everyone globally. The core of this argument is that we all aspire to increase our material wealth and that, as we progress through various stages of economic development, all members of all societies will ultimately achieve this goal. Some commentators point out how, just as members of society in developed economies have benefited from the growth of international trade in the nineteenth and twentieth centuries to become the consumer, so too those of the emerging economies of India, China, Brazil and other countries that trail in their wake will become the new consumers of the twenty-first century. But, with other critics, we question the morality and the impact of this new consumption.

We see two problems with conceptualizing people exclusively as consumers of the company's products and services. First, this implies that only those with sufficient disposable income deserve the attention of marketers, whilst, at a global level, there are hundreds of millions of people who are scarcely able to afford the basic necessities of life. As such, they are not spoken about within the discourse of IB, even though MNEs could play an important role in improving their situation. An example of this can be seen in the pharmaceutical industry, where new medicines are developed for wealthy markets, whereas many of the medicinal needs of citizens in poor countries remain unmet due to their low purchasing power. Second, the discourse of consumer orientation that pervades the IB literature implies that companies 'care' about the consumer, yet there are numerous examples of how business's concern for the 'good' of the consumer flies in the face of medical or scientific evidence.

It is only recently that some of the major food producers and supermarket chains have started to remove hydrogenated vegetable oils (also known as trans-fats) from their food products despite many years of research that shows their highly detrimental impact on human health. In addition, as controls over the sale of tobacco products have grown in the developed world, the tobacco companies have sought to develop new markets for their products in Africa and other parts of the world (see Goodchild and Hodgson, 2006). In a similar vein, in the face of international criticism and a report from the World Health Organization (WHO, 2006: 2) that says that 'optimal breastfeeding practices could avert 13% of the 10.6 million deaths of children under five years occurring globally every year', baby milk producers have pushed hard to develop new consumer groups in the less developed world through aggressive marketing of their infant milk formulas. Finally, China has seen an explosion in the manufacture and sale of cars over the last decade, with little or no concern from the investing multinational automobile manufacturers as to the environmental impact of the increasing emissions, whether upon the city dwellers of Shanghai and Beijing or on global greenhouse gas levels.

society and international business

As we have pointed out above, we wish to consider the effects of international business on society at large and, in particular, to raise issues of social and economic inequality and exploitation. To do this, we look first at some of the historical examples of such exploitation and how their legacy continues to this day. Early examples of IB include the transportation of entire populations from Africa to the Americas to be sold into slavery, to work on the cotton and tobacco plantations, or in service for the rich European settlers. Whilst the transportation of slaves was officially ended some 200 years ago, the descendants of those who were forcibly taken across the Atlantic Ocean from their homeland later provided a major part of the workforce of emerging US manufacturing industries. Whereas the slave trade developed around the Atlantic rim, in Asia, Europeans engaged in another form of international trade based upon exploitation and misery, in this case through trading opium. In the nineteenth century, two young Scottish entrepreneurs, whose names are carried forward to this day in the company Jardine Matheson Holdings, followed the lead of the East India Company and developed a highly profitable international business activity through 'importing' Indian opium into China to trade for Chinese teas and textiles. In the present day, we identify similar issues of the exploitation of groups in broad society where, as outlined above, people are seen as potential or actual consumers of a company's products and services, or as parts of the global workforce for their provision. In addition, globally, slavery still exists in the cities of the so-called developed world, from New York to London and in all major cities (see Bales, 2000).

In this book, we see the relationship between international businesses and members of society as going beyond the discourse of production and consumption. In particular, in our discussion of the wider impacts of IB, we point to the social and economic changes that have accompanied the development of economic globalization and the growth of MNEs. For example, we raise questions about the increasing economic stratification within and between societies and the emergence of global elites that represent the few real 'winners' from globalization.

In addition to issues of socio-economic exclusion and increasing poverty, we discuss cultural changes stemming from the availability of global products and the power of multinational brands. As early as 1899, Thorstein Veblen (1899/1995) coined the term 'conspicuous consumption' to describe how the rich of the time used commodities not for their utility value, but as expressions of their wealth. In the present day, we identify the drive of global brands to sell ever-greater amounts of their products through creating aspirations in the consumers to identify themselves with the brand. This is often achieved, not through direct marketing activity, but through sponsorship of sportsmen and women, pop stars, or even major events, in order to promote an emotional commitment by the consumer to the brand. Naomi Klein (2000) points to the extremes of such identification, where individuals are tattooed with the Nike 'swoosh', or commit murder in order to steal the latest branded trainers.

organization of this book

We have divided this book into three parts. In the first, we offer a speedy journey through time to show how the growth of today's MNEs, which operate at a global level, is linked to both a long line of IB practices and to the development of a range of theories of international trade and investment. We also present an overview of both those theories that are considered to be part of the canon of IB as a field of knowledge and those which are often excluded from discussions of the conceptual underpinnings of the discipline in mainstream textbooks. Further, we explain how contemporary IB theory and practice unproblematically assume that it is an activity that is 'good' for society in general and will ultimately benefit all members of humanity. In doing this, we also point out how proponents of IB ground their arguments in a selective reading of history and avoid consideration of some of the less glorious aspects of IB activity.

In the second part, we broaden our discussion to consider the role of a range of contemporary institutional frameworks underpinning IB and, in so doing, outline the various factors that contributed to their emergence and development over time. In particular, we address the role and status of institutions such as the International Monetary Fund (IMF), the World Bank and the World Trade Organization (WTO). We do this in order to facilitate understanding of the political and economic conditions underlying the growth of various structures of economic cooperation and integration between countries, such as the Association of South East Asian Nations (ASEAN) and the Common Market of the South (MERCOSUR). In engaging with different perspectives on the impact of these institutions, we open up a discussion of their role in the light of ongoing conditions of trade imbalance and global economic inequalities.

The third part of this book addresses the functional aspects of management in the international context, providing a broad overview of topics pertaining to the design and delivery of goods and services internationally: research and development (R&D), marketing, logistics and supply chain management. We also engage with aspects of finance, accounting and governance associated with IB transactions, as well as with issues relating to managing people in the international firm. In our approach to subjects typically falling under the umbrella of international management, we challenge some of the implicit assumptions that underpin the rhetoric of mainstream IB texts and present different perspectives on the implications and impacts of managerial practices.

Throughout this book, we seek to inspire your own critical reflection on the nature of IB in the world and, hopefully, to challenge you to consider the implications and impact of IB as it is currently constituted, with its drive for continual business growth and expansion as well as the actual and potential influence we all have on its future direction and purpose. It is not our intention to moralize, but we feel it is necessary to present ideas, practices, theories and critiques of IB from a range of perspectives beyond what we see as the largely 'business as usual' approach of mainstream IB textbooks, in order to stimulate reflection on why IB is as it is, and on how it might be different.

Part 1

Theories of International Trade and International Business

1

Classical and Neo-classical Theories of International Trade

introduction

In this chapter, we outline the historical context of IB as both a theoretical and a practical domain. To fully comprehend contemporary IB, we feel that some understanding of early theories of international trade is essential. So, we first seek to familiarize you with the chronological development and theoretical underpinnings of the discipline, in order to gain an understanding of how the current prevailing model of IB as a constituent of the neo-liberal globalization agenda has come to be. Through questioning often unstated assumptions behind theories of IB and through discussion of alternative perspectives on history and theory, we seek to promote thinking on a broader range of issues relating to the social, political and environmental impacts of IB practices. In particular, we hope to inspire you to question the neo-liberal globalization agenda that pervades much of the mainstream IB literature. In the present, the two main types of activity within IB are classified as 'international trade' and 'international investment'. Historically, international trade, involving commercial exchange of goods or services across boundaries, developed prior to international investment, that is the movement of capital between nations. Early theories of international trade that we address in this chapter include mercantilism, physiocratism, the theory of absolute advantage, the theory of comparative advantage, and the pure theory of trade. In addition, we discuss the early twentieth-century development of the theory of factor endowments. After presenting an overview of these theories and their practical implications, we discuss the challenges to them that arose from alternative thinking on socio-political issues at the end of the nineteenth century and in the early part of the twentieth century. These are, by and large, rooted in the writings of Karl Marx on the political economy.

the origins of international trade theory

International trade as a field of human endeavour has existed for millennia, and examples of what we now call 'IB transactions' can be traced back to the days of the Phoenician Empire. The earliest forms of IB were based on exchange of tangible goods, such as agricultural produce or luxury items like spices, silk and amber. The latter two gave their names to great trade routes that traversed continents: the Silk Road and the Amber Road. The first of these connected China with India, Mesopotamia, Persia, Egypt and Rome. The second provided a conduit for transporting amber from the North Sea and Baltic coasts across Europe to Italy, Greece, the Black Sea region and Egypt. As these trade routes developed in Europe and Asia, the indigenous peoples of Australasia and the Americas also travelled across land and sea to engage in the exchange of goods.

Whilst the origins of international trade as a practice were not confined to one geographical location, the theoretical foundations of contemporary IB are grounded in thinking that originated in Europe. From Columbus's arrival in the Americas in 1492, and even earlier, foundations were laid for the development of capitalism as a political-economic system that requires geographical expansion in order to create wider possibilities for capital accumulation, through enabling exploitation of resources and market opportunities beyond the home economy. Historically, with the rise of capitalism came theories explaining and legitimizing the need for countries to grow politically and economically beyond their original boundaries. The earliest theoretical foundations of the domain of IB are usually associated with the economic theory of 'mercantilism'. The development of mercantilism as the main school of economic thought in Europe from the sixteenth to the eighteenth century coincided with the move away from a feudal society, the emergence of the nation state, and colonial expansion of European powers during a period of global exploration and the 'discovery' of new lands. The rate of development accelerated from the seventeenth century with population growth, particularly in urban areas, and advancements in shipping, and then railway technology, that would provide the capability for the expansion of production and trade.

principles of mercantilism

The basic principle of mercantilism was that a state – understood as the government and the Treasury – should aim to maximize its wealth through one-way trade with other countries. This idea was underpinned by the economic principle of the 'zero sum game'. In relation to international trade, this meant that the country that exported finished products should be the beneficiary of any exchange, at the expense of the importer. As the country sought to maximize its exports, it aimed to keep its imports to a minimum, in order to support the accumulation of precious metals – the key measure of national wealth – by which it was paid for its exports.

Mercantilism represented the interests of governments and merchants engaged in this trade and, at the same time, it disadvantaged the labouring and farming classes. The ongoing social and economic poverty of these groups was seen as desirable, since any increase in their spending power, free time or levels of education was viewed as being at the expense of productivity, and hence as detrimental to the nation's economy.

Within the mercantile system, the growth in prosperity of one nation was also supported by application of selective export subsidies, coupled with import duties, tariffs and other restrictions imposed by the state. The employment of mercantilist trade principles in practice resulted in conflict between competing nation states, each seeking to gain control over land and resources and to secure the greatest share of what was considered a finite volume of trade in the world. Thus, the philosophy of mercantilism came to play a role in legitimizing the spread of European imperialism and sparked the outbreak of European wars between the sixteenth and eighteenth centuries. The war between France and the Netherlands of 1672 was held, in part at least, to be due to France's imposition of duties on a wide range of foreign goods, leading to Dutch retaliation in prohibiting the import of French wines, brandies and other goods.

Whilst mercantilism as an economic theory was dominant until supplanted by the ideas of Adam Smith, its flaws were recognized by some at an earlier date. Challenge to the principles of mercantilism, when it came, was not based upon a critical response to its privileging of some groups in society over others. Rather, it was developed by economists, based upon alternative ideas about how best to promote the economic good of the nation state. For example, early critics questioned the assumption of trade being a zero sum game and pointed to the possibility of both partners in an exchange benefiting from it. They also highlighted the weaknesses of some of the other theoretical assumptions of mercantilism, that we do not have the space to discuss here. What needs to be said is that, following these early criticisms of mercantilism, more comprehensive critiques of the mercantile system were offered by the French physiocrats and by the Scot, Adam Smith.

responses to mercantilism – physiocratism and Adam Smith's theory of absolute advantage

Today, we can recognize some influences of mercantilist practices in the application of protectionist policies by countries, including the USA, Japan and China, and by trading blocs such as the European Union. Despite the seemingly universal drive to trade liberalization and economic openness, governments will often act to promote exports, to discourage and reduce imports and, in some cases, will pursue a nationalist agenda and encourage the purchase of domestically produced goods. Historically, as early as the second half of the eighteenth century, the entire notion of the development of wealth through trade was rejected by the French 'physiocrats', who believed that a nation's wealth was generated by domestic agricultural production. In their economic theory, the physiocrats emphasized the role of farm workers as the 'productive' class, whom they distinguished from the 'proprietary' class of landowners and the 'sterile' class of artisans and merchants. The origin and popularity of physiocratism in France at this point in history is not surprising, since the country's economy was based upon agricultural rather than industrial production. It is worth noting that, contemporarily, the origins and reinforcement of the European Common Agricultural Policy in the second half of the twentieth century might be seen as the fall-out of the French historically favouring agriculture over manufacturing.

In the late eighteenth century, mercantilism ceased to be the dominant model of economic thinking and was superseded by the free market economics of Adam Smith (1776/1999), first set out in his seminal work *An Inquiry into the Nature and Causes of the Wealth of Nations*. When *The Wealth of Nations* was first published, Britain was the world's most highly developed capitalist economy, and the new industrial barons seized upon Smith's ideas about the necessity of freeing business from the shackles of government control. They saw his theories as enabling them to import raw materials without restriction and to expand their exports of manufactured goods without hindrance. At the same time, for the poor in society, Smith's free exchange gave the promise of access to cheap imports – in his time, specifically, grain. Smith's *Wealth of Nations* is generally regarded as the foundation of classical economics and as one of the most profound rationales for liberal, capitalist economics. As the most influential thinker in the history of capitalist economics, Smith's work had an impact on later economic theories, from those of Malthus and Ricardo, who built upon his thinking, to those of Karl Marx, who drew upon it in developing his critique of capitalism.

Smith's challenge to mercantilism was based on his view that government restrictions on economic freedom, such as tariffs and restrictive trade treaties, contributed to the increasing wealth of merchants, but constrained development and hence did not benefit the growing population at large. Indeed, Smith criticized most forms of governmental intervention in economic matters, believing that the role of government should be to provide educational, judicial, military and other institutional frameworks that were not profitable for private enterprise. Smith argued that individuals are driven by selfishness and greed and that, at the level of the whole economy, this will lead to a broader range of products and services being offered and to prices being driven down, with increased availability to the benefit of all. Smith referred to the mechanism through which this happens as the 'invisible hand' of the market, which balances production and the utilization of goods to the advantage of all. It is worth noting that, in his explanation of how the 'invisible hand' of the market works, Smith managed to make a link between greed and selfishness as motivators of human actions, and benefits for the whole society as the outcome of these actions – in other words, a link between the creation of profit and the generation of common good. The entire canon of classical economics is based upon this idea. However, as we will point out in many places in this book, the fact that over the years, more and more wealth has been generated globally has not meant that everybody's situation has improved. Indeed, millions of people nowadays starve, cannot afford healthcare and education for their families and more than a half of people globally live below the internationally defined poverty line of $2 per day (PRB, 2005). Moreover, both economic and social development indicators show that the situation for many in the world today has deteriorated over recent decades (Milanovic, 2005). This suggests that the capitalist system, rooted in the principles of economic freedom, has yet to deliver the promised common good. Nevertheless, it is important to discuss Smith's ideas regarding international trade exchange because of their historical and present-day impact.

Smith believed that replacing the restrictive mercantile system with free international exchange would lead to a reduction in levels of poverty and would stimulate social and moral improvement in all participating countries. His views on foreign trade were an extension of his principle that it is 'the maxim of every prudent master of a family, never to attempt to make at home what it will cost him more to make than buy'. Smith reasoned that countries should specialize in the production of goods for which they could achieve a low unit cost of production and import them if it was cheaper to do so than to produce them domestically. This reasoning underpins his 'theory of absolute advantage'. As Smith (1776/1999: 35) (somewhat optimistically) argued:

> By means of glasses, hotbeds and hot walls, very good grapes can be raised in Scotland, and very good wine too can be made of them at about thirty times the expense for which at least equally good wine can be brought from foreign countries. Would it be a reasonable law to prohibit the importation of all foreign wines merely to encourage the making of claret and burgundy in Scotland?'

Smith saw the possibility of all states gaining some form of advantage as a result of exporting goods that they could produce more efficiently than any other, whilst, at the same time, importing those for which an other country held 'absolute advantage' through its production efficiency. In general, he was against restrictions on trade and government intervention in the economy, except in a few instances where national security was held to be paramount.

Thinking about how Smith's ideas on international trade translate into contemporary conditions, let us take the example of comparing the production of aircraft by Boeing in the USA and Airbus in Europe with China's current dominance in the production of textiles. Whilst China is seen as having a large pool of low-cost labour, it currently lacks the necessary specialist resources for the efficient and effective production of commercial aircraft and, as such, the country offers a market to Boeing and Airbus for the export of passenger aircraft beyond their own domestic markets. At the same time, China's pool of labour does provide the essential key resource for the supply of low-cost textiles that have now taken a dominant position in the US and European domestic market. Viewed from the perspective of the theory of absolute advantage, both developments are perceived as 'beneficial' in meeting consumer demand in the most cost-effective manner. We must, of course, remember that in using this example, we, like Smith, do not take account of the broader context in which the exchange takes place. For example, rather than stating that through trade exchange of aircraft and textiles both the USA and China benefit, we may ask who exactly in both countries draws benefits from this trade, what implications this has for parties in other countries, and how it influences environmental conditions globally.

As we mentioned above, Smith's theory assumed that the invisible hand of the market would ultimately lead to benefit for every member of society. The basic principles of this economic liberalism were subject to challenge and critique by Karl Marx and others from the second half of the nineteenth century. We will return to these arguments later in the chapter.

beyond Smith – theory of comparative advantage

Despite the impact of Smith's work, it was not devoid of critical response from others. Early critics argued that examples of absolute advantage are rare, since few countries possess a monopolistic hold over the production capability for any given commodity. In addition, some critics pointed out that Smith had not considered the situation where two countries might both benefit from trade exchange with each other even where one holds absolute advantage over the other in the production of all goods. This situation is addressed in the 'theory of comparative advantage', first referred to in Robert Torrens' (1815) *Essay on the*

External Corn Trade and formalized by David Ricardo (1817) through a numerical example provided in his book *On the Principles of Political Economy and Taxation.* Whilst the theory of comparative advantage has become one of the most important concepts in international trade theory, it has remained one of the most commonly misunderstood. We realize that for those who have not previously had much exposure to economic theory, an attempt to grasp the logic of the theory of comparative advantage may not, at first sight, seem like a very exciting task. However, as this part of international trade theory informs the understanding both of later developments and of much of the critique of these, we will now spend some time explaining the logic behind it in simple terms. In doing this, we wish to stress the significance of two concepts: 'opportunity cost' and 'comparative advantage'.

Ricardo's example refers to a hypothetical situation in which there are only two countries (for convenience called England and Portugal), two goods being produced (cloth and wine) and only one factor of production, namely labour. Whilst Smith only considered the possibility that each of the countries was more productive in one of the commodities than the other, Ricardo addressed the situation in which one – Portugal – was more efficient in the production of both. For Smith, such a situation could not be seen as resulting in an advantageous exchange for England. However, Ricardo showed that, despite Portugal's advantage in both goods, it remains possible for both countries to benefit from trade exchange, where each country specializes in the production of one of them. He also considered that the overall supply of both products would increase, compared to the situation before specialization and trade. According to this reasoning, the choice of which commodity each country should specialize in is not determined by a simple comparison of the costs of production between countries, as defined by the cost of labour. Rather, as Ricardo argued, it is necessary to consider the 'opportunity costs' of producing both goods in both countries. The opportunity cost of, say, producing cloth versus wine is the amount of wine that must be sacrificed in order to free resources for the production of a unit of cloth. If, for example, Portugal is twice as efficient as England in the production of cloth, but three times as efficient in the production of wine, then it has comparative advantage in wine. At the same time, however, if England must relinquish less wine than would Portugal in order to manufacture one additional unit of cloth, it holds comparative advantage over Portugal in the production of cloth. Following this logic, if Portugal specializes and trades in the goods for which it is '*most better*' than England in production efficiency, and England focuses on producing that for which it is '*least worse*' than Portugal, both countries can benefit from specialization and exchange.

Whilst Ricardian theory can explain how things *might* happen in an ideal world, there are several problematic assumptions that underpin it. Some of these are of a theoretical nature, such as the assumptions about the existence of only two countries, labour being the only factor of production, and the trade exchange taking place under conditions of perfect competition. Perhaps more crucially, we would take issue with the major ideological assumptions that Ricardian thinking shares with the ideas of Adam Smith, that is that economic activity driven by the desire to generate profits will bring about positive outcomes for everybody in society.

the impact of history on contemporary IB practice

In case you wonder what purpose these historical accounts serve, beyond outlining the origins and evolution of international trade theory, we would draw your attention to the fact that early theorizations of economic protectionism and liberalism, as exemplified in mercantilism and the ideas of Adam Smith, are linked to specific instruments of government trade policy that have not only played an important role historically, but remain of significance at the present time. Moreover, these classical theories underpin the current dominant paradigm that sees international business as an inherently 'good' project and, as such, these early theories give insights into fundamental assumptions that underpin contemporary international business theory and practice. They have also informed a range of developments in organization and management over time.

If we consider how mercantile ideas are used to provide legitimization for protectionist policies by nations, we can identify them as underpinning the most common justifications of government intervention in international trade, namely the protection of infant industries and the promotion of industrialization, the protection of jobs – particularly those that are lower paid and require lower skill levels – in the domestic market, consumer protection – especially for reasons of health and safety, and the protection of national interests. This final category encapsulates action in supporting industries considered as being of strategic importance, such as defence suppliers, or those that have the potential of becoming globally competitive, as well as government implementation of foreign policy, and protection of national identity and culture.

If we look more closely at specific instruments that underpin policies of international trade, both historically and contemporarily, we see that nation states have applied both 'tariff' and 'non-tariff' tools. The former are represented by import duties, whereby government places a tax on foreign produce. As a result, its price is raised above that at which the home country supplier provides it. Since the imported goods become more expensive compared to the domestically produced equivalent, consumers are more likely to purchase goods delivered by home-country firms, and hence, domestic producers are protected from foreign competition. At the same time, the government of the country benefits from duties paid on those goods that are imported. In recent years, the Scotch Whisky industry has fought for the reduction of import duty rates in other countries, such as India and Japan, where the governments of these countries have applied high rates of import duty in order to protect domestic producers.

Non-tariff barriers include import quotas, voluntary export restraints (VERs) and subsidies. Import quotas restrict the amount of a specified product that may be brought into the country, again generally to offer a degree of protection to domestic producers. Recent examples of quota application include Japan's and South Korea's restrictions on the importation of rice. Whilst quotas are applied by importing nations, VERs are implemented by the exporter through a bilateral agreement with the target market government. The most commonly quoted application of VERs relates to the limits on exportation of automobiles from Japan to various western countries in the 1980s and 1990s, with the aim of protecting uncompetitive home industries in these countries. Governments may provide subsidies in order to promote the competitiveness of domestic industries in export markets, or to protect their domestic market position. In recent times, the issue of agricultural subsidies has been the subject of intergovernmental wrangles and accusation and counter-accusation. The European Union has claimed that the USA subsidizes its wheat industry excessively, whilst the USA argues that the European Common Agricultural Policy (CAP) similarly favours European farmers. In both cases, the argument is that domestic producers are protected from external competition by being enabled to continue with production that would otherwise be economically non-viable. As the EU and USA accuse each other of unfair practices, so non-governmental organizations (NGOs) say that both protect their home agribusiness, thereby excluding access to markets by developing countries whilst, at the same time, enabling overproduction of commodities that are then 'dumped' in developing countries to the detriment of their own farmers.

Similarly to mercantilism, classical economics also continues to influence policies and practices within contemporary IB. In developing his theory of absolute advantage, Smith grounded his thinking in the 'labour theory' of value – that the value of any good is a function of the amount of labour expended in its production – and he expounded the idea of the division of labour as a way of increasing production efficiency. In contrast to craft production, where a craftsman would produce a complete commodity, the division of labour involves splitting production of the commodity into discrete elements, each of which is completed by a different semi-skilled worker. Smith expanded this reasoning from consideration of individual specialization to that of whole nations. His ideas have underpinned a vast array of changes in trade and industry, with a rapid acceleration of key trends in the second half of the twentieth century. After the Second World War, the emergence and growth of 'new' economies, particularly in South East Asia, was linked to the decline of traditional production industries in developed economies. This trend was seen first in the UK, then across Europe, despite the continuing existence – to start with, at least – of expertise and the means of production. A prime example of this can be seen in the area of shipbuilding, where the UK was the world leader through the nineteenth and early twentieth centuries. However, as the new economies built up their human and material production resources, they proceeded to undercut the production costs of UK shipbuilding, whilst maintaining the quality necessary to ship owners. Both Japan and South Korea contributed to the virtual demise of a UK industry that had dominated the world, and the riverfronts of major cities such as Belfast, Glasgow and Newcastle.

The theory of comparative advantage, with its main argument that international trade can increase the welfare of all countries, continues to influence the thinking of those individuals and agencies that promote the need for ever-increasing transnational trade and investment. Despite its unrealistic assumptions, the principles of Ricardian theory have been used to argue that specialization and free trade are beneficial since they lead to improvements in production and consumption efficiency. In addition, they have been deployed to suggest that less developed economies can compete in the global marketplace through seeking to identify and exploit those areas in which they hold comparative advantage over developed economies. Such exhortations, however, ignore the reality of a world in which the power and impact of political and economic agents are inescapable. In the contemporary world of international trade, even 'low cost' economies now lose out to 'even lower' cost areas of production. Garment producers in Sri Lanka, whose work was drawn from the transfer of production

from the UK, now find themselves unemployed as business is moved
to India and China. Similarly, the shipbreakers of Chittagong in
Bangladesh (see Chapter 2 for more on this) now fear for the loss
of their jobs to China, with its high demand for steel.

Despite the apparent negative impacts of the loss of jobs and
industries, the basic implication of classical theories of international trade is that, thanks to exchange, more wealth will be created and consumption levels will increase, and will be able to do
so beyond the limits of possibility for domestic production alone.
Whilst questions about how to tackle poverty and inequality
within and between nations remain unanswered at a more specific
level by the classical trade theories, the prospects of general wealth
creation and higher consumption levels are unproblematically
viewed as a worthy cause, and as a motivator for capitalist development and for countries' engagement in international trade.
Only in recent years, with the realization of the global impact of
pollution, resource depletion and climate change, has this assumption been challenged by those working within the paradigm.

neo-classical trade theories – the theory of pure trade

To this point, the theories of trade that we have discussed were
all based on the economics of supply, with the assumption that
the value of commodities was dependent upon the cost of labour
involved in their production. The French economist Jean Baptiste
Say (1803/2001) was the first to move away from the labour theory of value, laying the ground for what later became known as
'equilibrium analysis'. In its advanced form, in 'neo-classical economics' developed by Jevons (1871), Menger (1871/1950) and
Walras (1874) during the second half of the nineteenth century,
we find the first suggestion that the price of a commodity is determined not only by the costs of production, but also by the 'utility'
obtained by the consumer. Consumers are recognized as making
choices of whether or not to buy any particular product at a given
price and, through such choices, to influence the allocation of

resources by producers in search of efficiency maximization. In relation to international exchange, neo-classical economics embraced the 'pure theory of trade', first expounded by Alfred Marshall (Marshall and Marshall, 1879/1994), which promoted a free market and open competition, and which incorporated consideration of both producer and consumer behaviour.

Pure trade theory introduced the idea of 'consumer preferences' into a discussion of international trade. Analytically, it relied upon the use of mathematics in developing quantitative models of exchange. Geometric diagrams were used to show how gains from international trade could be achieved by the trading parties. Here, it is not our intention to explain the mathematical formulae behind the models of exchange grounded in the pure theory of trade. Those of you interested in its exposition and content may wish to read about it elsewhere (e.g. Ietto-Gillies, 2005). What is important here is to recognize how, despite a greater theoretical sophistication, neo-classical trade theories are grounded in the same assumption as the classical ones, that is that capitalist development under the conditions of the free market economy – including the liberalization of trade – will serve the general interests of the entire society. On a theoretical level, this problematic is addressed by more recent writings stemming from the Marxist tradition, to which we will return in the next chapter.

theory of factor endowments

The final stage of development of country-based theories of international trade was Heckscher (1919/1950) and Ohlin's (1933/1967) 'theory of factor endowments'. Heckscher and Ohlin argued that comparative advantage of one country over another in the production of a given commodity stems from the relative abundance of the factor that is more intensely utilized in its production. In its original form, the model assumed only two factors of production (labour and capital), two commodities and two countries (2×2×2). Based upon this basic model, if one country has an abundance of labour relative to the other, it will export labour-intensive goods, whereas if it is relatively labour-scarce, it will import these. Likewise, if it is relatively capital-rich, it will concentrate its exports in those products that require high capital input. The initial version of the Heckscher–Ohlin theory, with its simplistic reliance on the 2×2×2 framework, was later developed to incorporate more realistic assumptions, such as the introduction of further factors of production (e.g. land) and consideration of the role of tariffs in shaping patterns of international trade.

The Heckscher–Ohlin theory has been very influential in international economics because of the explanation it offers to the question about the source of comparative advantage, moving beyond the classical labour theory of value and enabling a range of factors of production to be considered. However, despite its strong appeal at a theoretical level, the underpinning assumptions of the theory of factor endowments have turned out to be problematic and, at an empirical level, its relevance has been limited. Nevertheless, faced with the option of rejecting factor endowments theory or seeking to explain its failings, many economists have followed the latter route, being unwilling to give up its high theoretical significance within neo-classical economics.

Whilst the results of these attempts have been inconclusive, we would highlight issues of relevance to understanding contemporary international business, stemming from assumptions inherent in the Heckscher–Ohlin model. For example, the model assumes perfect competition in factor and production markets, and lacks consideration of transportation costs. Neither of these conditions holds in contemporary IB practice that is characterized by powerful multinational players and a global logistics network. Moreover, the Heckscher–Ohlin model is based upon the premise that both capital and labour are mobile domestically, but immobile between countries. In the modern business world, barriers to the movement of capital have been reduced and, with the advent of the Internet and electronic transactions, capital can be moved across the world in milliseconds. Whilst, at present, labour is not as internationally mobile as capital, labour migration is seen across the world now and was taking place both at the time when Heckscher and Ohlin were developing their theory and over centuries before. Finally, as with classical theories and the remaining neo-classical ones, the model is rooted in the assumption that free market competition and international exchange are good and beneficial for all within the nations involved in them. In the rest of this book, we will show how, in the contemporary world of IB activity and in its representation in mainstream IB textbooks, this assumption remains central to the development of MNEs and to the institutions and practices of IB. We will illustrate how the neo-liberal model of globalization and IB that predominates at the present time perpetuates the principles of free trade and the ideology that the freer and more unfettered the market is for business, the greater the benefits to be accrued to all.

critiques of classical and neo-classical trade theories

So far in this chapter we have sought to provide an overview of the early theories of international trade, since these constitute the conceptual underpinnings of contemporary IB. We have specifically engaged with the following theoretical developments: mercantilism, physiocratism, theory of absolute advantage, theory of comparative advantage, and pure theory of trade. We have drawn attention to the links between early theoretical developments on international trade within the discipline and the broader historical, political, social and economic contexts in which they took place. In particular, we have highlighted the central role of European nation states as the dominant actors in international political economy. These nation states sought to maximize their wealth through accumulation, first, of precious metals and, later, through trade exchange with other countries. The ideas of the mercantilists and, subsequently, of Adam Smith and other proponents of free markets and unrestrained trade provided an appealing theoretical justification for the realization of these objectives. They also justified the expansionist aspirations of European powers in terms of a projected increase in wealth and other benefits for all, across all involved countries. The betterment provided by these benefits was, however, relative to the individual's previous state and the existence and perpetuation of inequalities between groups was seen not only as unproblematic but as necessary.

Classical theories of international trade, with their assumptions of the desirability of exchange and the accumulation of wealth, coincided with and underpinned the growth of capitalism as the dominant economic system. In contrast to mediaeval feudalism, in which ownership of land was the major indicator of wealth, for the new merchant classes and the bourgeoisie who emerged as the implementers and beneficiaries of international trade, the key measure of wealth became ownership of financial capital and of the means of production. Over time, the central tenet of capitalism has been the need for growth and this was seen to be sustained by geographic expansion through the processes of colonization and imperialism. The colonization process was made possible through developments in technology and logistics, but it was driven primarily by government aspirations and actions. Whilst the history of, say, the British Empire is generally written as one of heroic discovery, civilization and progress, critical commentators provide accounts of endemic violence, exploitation and the ignoring of many generations of indigenous culture and civilization. They point to the continuing legacy of this hegemony in contemporary theories of business, management and organization.

In most IB texts, the classical and neo-classical approaches to international trade tend to be presented and summarized in terms of the rhetoric of growth and benefit. In these texts, it is difficult, if not impossible, to discern any critical discussion that seeks to challenge this fundamental tenet – or to point out that, in reality, international trade does not take place under the conditions of perfect competition. Within the canon of IB textbooks, there is little or no mention of alternative views on economics in general and international exchange in particular, such as, for example, Marxism and its argumentation against the supposed ubiquitous social benefits of capitalism. We would suggest that, even in a very short book about international business, some mention of the theoretical alternative to classical and neo-classical economics is needed in order to create space for a critique of IB through references to empirical examples. Here, Marx's writing is of particular significance since it originates from the first half of the nineteenth century, during the period when free market economics dominated trade theory development, and since his ideas have been carried forward into much of the later critical thinking on political economy and society. Below, we offer a brief background to the ideas of Marx and a few other writers from the Marxist tradition, including Hobson, Lenin and Bukharin. The Marxist perspective draws attention to the fact that free market policies create conditions in which the monopolistic tendencies of capitalist enterprises can be realized. In addition, it highlights the fact that not every party wins in trade exchange. At the level of international economy, it shows that some nations will derive benefits whilst others will be exploited. The same phenomenon can be observed at the country level, where some in society will increase their wealth at the expense of others.

the Marxist response

Karl Marx was one of the major critics not of IB *per se*, but of the social, political and economic structures that underpin capitalism. For Marx, the growth of international trade was an inherent element in the development of capitalism and the emergence of the 'bourgeoisie'. Whilst Smith argued for increasing production and trade of commodities for the benefit of all in society, Marx (with Friedrich Engels) saw trade as the vehicle for accumulation of capital by the new bourgeoisie through the exploitation of the working class. Marx and Engels (1848/2002) did not see the internationalization of production and exchange in terms of their aggregate outputs of increased production and consumption efficiency, but rather as manifestations of power in society. They, as well as later Marxist writers, associated the development of international trade with imperialism and colonization, and questioned the assumption that this trade is an inherently desirable project. Following Marx, in his book *Imperialism*, John Hobson (1902/1938) proposed that Britain's drive to develop its Empire did not result in increased wealth and improvement for the majority of its population. Rather, he argued that, contrary to perceived wisdom on the benefits of trade with its Empire, the overall social and economic costs of imperialism, even within Britain itself, far outweighed any advantages from expansion. On the basis of this assertion, Hobson (1902/1938: 46) asked the question, 'How is the British nation induced to embark upon such unsound business?' In response, he himself offered the following explanation: 'The only possible answer is that the business interests of the nation as a whole are subordinated to those of certain sectional interests that usurp control of the national resources and use them for their private gain.' The sectional interests that he identified were those of the educated middle and upper classes with appropriate skills and resources, but with the primary role being that of the financial investors.

Hobson countered classical economic theories' assertions of the possibility of achievement of benefits for all in society through trade by highlighting increased social and economic stratification. In a similar vein, Vladimir Ilich Lenin (1902/1969) argued that, rather than taking place under conditions of perfect competition, internationalization of production inevitably leads to the emergence of monopolies and inequality of power, characterized by the privileged position of the bourgeoisie over the working class. As organizations grow and develop home market monopolies, prospects for the generation of profits in this domestic market decrease. In search of new opportunities, geographic expansion takes place through colonization and the exploitation of resources in the colonized territories. In this way, surplus capital from the saturated domestic market is invested in order to create further economic growth and returns.

In contrast to the assumptions of classical and neo-classical theories – that international trade is a process of mutual benefit between nations – Lenin's argument points to it being one of exploitation of the colonized nations. The colonizers are seen as gaining advantage both from the importation of commodities from their colonies and from their investment in new infrastructure and development projects in them. Here, the productive resources of the colonies are appropriated by and absorbed into the capitalist enterprises of the colonizing nation. As such, for Lenin, international trade is first and foremost driven by the interests of capitalists and primarily benefits them. Lenin predicted that the increasing fragmentation and stratification of society would lead to growing conflict and to revolution and the overthrow of capitalism. Building upon Lenin's ideas, the topic of international trade was addressed by Nikolai Bukharin (1917/1987) in relation to the international division of labour. According to Bukharin, this international division would lead to the development of strong links between both capitalists and workers across national boundaries. Whilst we might argue that the former is evident in contemporary society, with the rise of MNEs and the mobility of the wealthy as members of a new 'global elite', we would posit that there are at present few signs of effective cross-border organization of the labour movement.

▨▨▨▨▨ conclusion

In this chapter, we have sought to place our discussion of the historical antecedents of IB into a broader theoretical context, to point to some of the problematic aspects of international trade and IB that are usually neglected in the mainstream literature, but which can be identified as inherent in both historical and contemporary practices. As we have explained above, since the writings of Adam Smith, promotion of the doctrine of free trade between nations has been central to classical and neo-classical theories. In practice, the take-up of this doctrine by individual countries has been, at best, patchy, and closely allied to the broader context surrounding the different economic and political circumstance that prevailed. Whilst Britain was at the centre of the nineteenth-century free trade movement, lowering tariffs by 20% in the years from 1840 to 1880, some economic historians have argued that this happened not so much under the influence of the thinking of Smith and others, but because government was able to raise funds through other means, in particular, through income tax drawn from the expanding population working in its burgeoning industries.

Other European countries did not adopt universal free trade principles and, in supporting international trade development, relied to a great extent upon reciprocal trade agreements with preferred partners, known as 'most favoured nations' (MFNs). By the late 1860s, such agreements had been adopted by the majority of European nations. Even though MFN status involved the liberalization of trade, it was often conferred for political rather than purely economic reasons. France, for example, entered into a bilateral free trade agreement with Prussia with the intention of acting against the interests of Austria-Hungary. As European nations moved towards freer trade regimes, the United States remained more protectionist and continued to maintain import duties on a wide variety of products up to the 1880s.

Whilst European bilateral trade pacts were negotiated on a partnership basis, both Britain and the United States used gunboat diplomacy to force open markets in Asia. After the first Opium War with China, Britain initially occupied Hong Kong, then negotiated its ceding from China to Britain. After the second Opium War, Britain set up free trade in Chinese ports such as Shanghai. Similarly, the USA sent Commodore Matthew Perry's fleet of 'black ships' to force Japan to abandon its closed economy, to end a 200-year exclusive trading partnership with the Netherlands, and to engage in free trade exchange with the USA under the 1854 Treaty of Peace and Amity.

From these examples we can see how, historically, the liberalization of trade did not necessarily proceed in a peaceful manner, based on all parties' understanding that it would bring benefits for all, but that coercion through military action had an important role to play in its spread. In conclusion, in this brief historical overview we posit that, in order to understand how the conditions in which contemporary IB practices take place developed, it is necessary to be aware of the classical and neo-classical theories of international trade. In addition, if we are to critically appraise these theories and the impact of practices legitimized by them at a societal level, it is essential to have an understanding of the historical context in which these theories were built. Finally, we have seen the need for an acquaintance with alternative theories that challenge the underpinning logic of classical and neo-classical economics, and the circumstances in which, historically, the doctrine of free trade was implemented as the principle of trade between countries.

2

Twentieth-century Developments in Trade Theories and IB Practice

▨▨▨▨▨ introduction

In this chapter, we consider the development of more recent theories of IB in the twentieth century, and their relationship to emerging forms of IB practice. The key change of focus that occurred in thinking about IB was a move from nation states as the key actors in IB to the emergence of the firm as the central player. As we will discuss, the more recent theories that underpin international trade address the subject of how to generate maximum profits for the company and its shareholders. We will consider how, in so doing, they subordinate the interests of other stakeholders to those of the firm. In this way, we will see how, for example, issues of differential earning power across nations are viewed not as problematic, but as offering new sources of competitive advantage to the MNE.

The specific theories that we address in this chapter are: preference similarity theory, product life cycle theory, new trade theory, strategic trade theory, and the model of the competitive advantage of nations. As in Chapter 1, we also introduce some of the critical arguments that counter the tenets of mainstream IB literature.

the changing environment of international business

In the latter part of the nineteenth century, a lengthy phase of continuous growth in world trade had been followed by economic slowdown and a decline in trade activity. As a response to the changing economic climate and to pressures from internal producers, country after country introduced punitive tariffs on imported commodities. For example, to protect the livelihood of their farmers, European governments had closed their markets to imports of grain from Ukraine and the USA. Similarly, in Germany, Chancellor Otto Bismarck had introduced tariffs in response to demands from landowners and industrialists, whilst in France the punitive Méline Tariff was imposed on imports in 1892. In the New World, having been slow to open its markets, the United States had become one of the most protectionist nations, providing a cushion for its infant manufacturing industries as the country sought to recover from the economic impact of the Civil War.

Early in the twentieth century, this economic decline was brought to a temporary halt by the outbreak of the First World War, which stimulated growth and investment – primarily in the manufacture of instruments of war and in technological development of new weapons systems. After the First World War and a phase of growth in the 1920s, the course of economic decline resumed and culminated in the Great Depression that started in 1929 and continued for most of the 1930s. Throughout this period, governments across the world engaged in a new round of protectionist interventions and the imposition of tariffs and quotas. During the 1930s, the level of international trade dropped by between 20% and 38% for individual nations and by 1950 trade, as a share of national output, was at a lower level than it had been prior to the First World War.

Whilst our overview of history shows that, at a theoretical level, policies of free trade have been advocated since the time of Adam Smith, it also demonstrates that in almost two centuries, they had not found a place on the official agenda of most governments.

Moreover, as we ponder our current situation, with institutions expounding the rhetoric of ever-freer trade and with the emergence of common markets and trading blocs, we must remember that international business today does not operate in a free market context. To appreciate the extent of contemporary constraints within IB, it is necessary to move beyond consideration of the role of governments in shaping the global business environment, and to take account of the significance and impact of companies in the development of more recent theories of IB. This has been reflected in the advancement of 'firm-based' theories that attempt to explain the nature of trade patterns across the world. Moreover, these theories move away from an almost exclusive emphasis on the role of a country's factor endowments as determinants of trade, and instead draw greater attention to the role of the demand side in explaining international trade patterns.

preference similarity theory

One of the first theories that considered the importance of both firms and the demand side for an understanding of trade exchange between countries was developed by Steffan Linder (1961) and is referred to as 'preference similarity theory' (Hufbauer, 1970). In his *Essay on Trade and Transformation*, Linder challenged Heckscher and Ohlin's focus on factors of production as the key determinants of exchange between nations. Seeking to explain trading patterns and partnerships – in particular, in relation to similar goods and between countries at a comparable level of economic development – Linder argued that actual trade depends upon factors that strengthen it, the so-called 'trade-creating forces', and those that hinder it, 'trade-braking forces'. He believed that the development of international trade arose from strengths in domestic demand and production, whereby a country would export those commodities for which it already had a strong home market. From this, he argued that the major trade-creating forces would be grounded in similarities of demand, based upon per capita income and consumer preferences, as determined by both economic and non-economic factors.

The trade-braking factors, on the other hand, were specified by Linder as being caused by the use of scarce factors in the demanded goods, physical distance, or barriers to trade erected by governments. The implications of Linder's theory are that consumers in countries with a comparable level of income and with similar culture, climate, etc. will purchase similar goods, irrespective of whether or not they are made in their homeland. Following Linder's explanation of the underlying logic of intra-industry trade, and barring any trade-braking factors, a consumer in Germany, for example, will consider buying red wine from the Bordeaux, Chianti, Rheinhessen or Rioja regions and so, wine producers in France, Italy, Germany and Spain will all have access to the German market.

Various empirical studies have been undertaken to test Linder's theory and the results of these are inconclusive. Some studies have supported Linder's proposition and have extended it beyond his original claim that it applied only to high-income countries, presenting evidence for its application to trade between 'less developed countries' (LDCs). Other writers, however, have questioned the strength of the trade-creating factors, and have pointed to the importance of geographical proximity as a major determinant of trade patterns. Leaving aside the disputed degree of accuracy of Linder's theory at an empirical level, we would point to the fact that it is mainly concerned with attempting to answer the question of which countries a firm can and should sell its products in, rather than with exploring whether and under what circumstances international business activities of companies are beneficial for society as a whole.

product life cycle theory

Raymond Vernon (1966), a key figure in a number of developments in post-Second World War international business, proposed 'product life cycle theory', focusing on the life cycle and trade of products. Vernon was a member of the team that developed the Marshall Plan – the post-Second World War US plan for supporting European reconstruction whilst, at the same time, resisting the spread of Soviet communism. He was also involved in the founding of the International Monetary Fund (IMF) and the General Agreement on Tariffs and Trades (GATT), the forerunner of the current World Trade Organization (WTO). Vernon's product life cycle theory describes the three stages of the cycle: from new product development, into maturity, and from there to standardization. At the development stage, a new product is generally produced and exported by the country in which it has originated through research and development (R&D). As it becomes accepted into the international marketplace, production will be started up in other countries in order to meet the new demand. As production becomes widespread, manufacture will become concentrated in areas of greatest efficiency, with the result that the commodity ends up being exported back into the country where it was first conceived. Vernon's theory tends to be used to explain how, for example, the initial invention, technological development and production of many electronic goods was undertaken in Europe or the United States, and how the countries involved developed early export trades in these products. However, in recent times, the manufacturing and export of such goods has been concentrated in LDCs, whilst the original producers concentrate their efforts on developing further innovations.

Through describing how production of technologically advanced goods transfers from country to country, Vernon's model seems to imply that all countries have the opportunity to benefit from any innovation, regardless of where it originated. However, as some commentators have pointed out (e.g. Arrighi et al., 2003), Vernon's theory and mainstream interpretations and representations of it fail to address the complexity of the socio-economic implications of technology and production transfer over time. Vernon admits that the innovation process generally begins in advanced economies, but he does not engage with the fact that, as a consequence of this, these countries will derive maximum benefit from the early-stage, higher profits, thereby adding to their wealth. As production increases and is spread out into the LDCs, both the unit cost of production and profit levels decline markedly. As a result, the poorer countries derive a much lesser return from their involvement in the spread of the original innovation.

Critics argue that successful exploitation and wealth maximization from one innovation enables the already rich countries to accumulate both the financial and intellectual capital to fund further cycles of R&D and new product development, and hence, to generate above-average profits. Less developed countries, however, remain bound to the low-profit, mass-production stage. Whilst this allows them to participate in industrialization, this does not translate into enabling them to increase their level of economic development in line with that of the developed countries. This self-reinforcing cycle of a specific geographical organization of diminishing profits from innovation contributes to ever-greater economic stratification at a global level and to the perpetuation of the 'north–south' divide. At the present time, the extremes of the innovation/production separation are manifest in the proliferation of low-cost manufacturing in export processing zones (EPZs) and other tax- and regulation-free facilities, a subject to which we will return later.

new trade theory

The firm-based theories that we have discussed so far all assume that the organization is working in a perfectly competitive market, and they do not engage with the question of competition between rival companies. The incorporation of 'imperfect' competitive conditions into models of trade was developed by Paul Krugman (1979, 1981) in his 'new trade theory'. Krugman pointed out that, even within competitive markets with a high number of different players, some firms will have an influence over the industry price structures. These companies will be ones that have succeeded in growing faster than their competitors and achieving economies of scale. As such, they will enjoy a degree of monopoly power within the market. Through engaging in international trade, these firms are able to increase the overall size of the market they serve and, as a result of exploitation of economies of scale, they will generate monopoly profits. The possibility of earning such monopoly profits will, of course, form an attractive proposition for potential new market entrants and, as such, might lead to increased competitive rivalry. In order to minimize the threat to their own business from both new and existing competitors, firms will develop specialization within a given product range. Where such specialization is undertaken by a number of companies from different countries, there will be an overall increase in the types of similar but differentiated products offered. As a result, consumers in all countries will be able to avail themselves of a wider choice of goods produced by firms in the same industry, and there will be growth in intra-industry trade between countries.

Krugman's major contribution to the theory of trade was to move away from the assumption of perfect competition, and to incorporate the notion of economies of scale as a factor motivating firms to engage in producing goods not only for domestic but also for international markets. Krugman's theory addresses the growth imperative of organizations that seek to dominate their domestic market and to expand internationally. For example, it can be used to explain the case of Boeing and Airbus, both of which have grown through merger and acquisition and by establishing dominance in their home markets, but now compete against each other at a global level, including within each other's domestic market. However, Krugman's model excludes the influence of a number of factors – such as geographical distance, the role of government and the existence of trade blocs – upon overall trade patterns. The significance of one such factor – the role of government – is specifically addressed in 'strategic trade theory', which explores the possible range of impacts of government intervention under the circumstances of imperfect competition. We do not have space here to discuss this in theory detail, but an explanation of it can be found, for example, in Ietto-Gillies (2005).

Krugman's theory offers explanations for the actions of companies and suggests that firms will seek to grow internationally in order to take advantage of economies of scale and to win market share from their competitors. It addresses the question of what a firm would consider as 'good' from the point of view of profit generation. However, it does not problematize the way in which this drive towards geographic expansion and achievement of a monopoly position (i.e. domination over other entities) impacts upon the rest of the stakeholders in this paradigm of IB.

competitive advantage of nations

One of the leading thinkers on management in the late twentieth century, Michael Porter, has contributed a key model to contemporary understanding of aspects of IB relating to choice of business location. This model, which enables consideration of *The Competitive Advantage of Nations* (Porter, 1990), is referred to as 'Porter's Diamond'. The diamond incorporates four key attributes of country-specific conditions that shape the business environment, making countries more or less competitive as targets of business activity at an international level. These attributes are: (1) factor endowments, (2) demand conditions, (3) related and supporting industries, and finally, (4) business strategy, structure and rivalry. The first of these refers to a country's productive capabilities, such as its pool of skilled labour, its natural resources and its infrastructure.

To Porter, the workforce may constitute a source of competitive advantage not only in terms of the available skill levels, but also, in relation to the cost of employment. As such, some countries are seen as attractive locations for establishing operations as long as they are able to offer a bountiful supply of cheap labour, coupled with other factors that are favourable to the investing company. In contemporary global business, this is exemplified by the emergence of entities such as 'export processing zones' that offer tax-free imports and exports, subsidies for the establishment of facilities and infrastructure and, in the most extreme cases, exemption from any labour controls and employment laws. The existence of these zones allows companies to reduce their operating costs and, to some commentators, provides a foundation for economic growth and development. For others (e.g. Klein, 2000), however, the search for ever-cheaper production costs and the ability of organizations to move operations at will across the globe is seen as contributing to a 'race to the bottom'.

The second attribute in Porter's diamond – demand conditions – describes the quality and quantity of demand for a given type of product in companies' home markets. According to Porter, it is the relative strength of demand and the discerning nature of consumers in this market that gives firms the competitive edge that enables them to compete successfully in international markets and other countries. For example, the seeds of Japanese consumer electronics firms' global dominance were planted in a highly competitive home market, in which an ever-more affluent middle class was willing and able to purchase newly developed and technologically-advanced products. For Porter, it is not the size of the market, but the crucial element of 'character' that is important.

The third attribute is that of related and supporting industries. All organizations are parts of networks in which they rely upon other firms to supply components, raw materials, or different types of support services to them. The presence of these supplementary organizations, and whether or not they are competitive at an international level, will be a key factor considered when the firm is assessing possible business locations. Traditionally, the location of these supporting industries would have been looked at in terms of geographic proximity. However, in the age of global logistics and telecommunications and the advent of the Internet, other factors will be taken into account. Nowadays, MNEs establish global networks of suppliers based upon their ability to provide relevant capabilities on the most advantageous business terms.

In contemporary business, issues of cost and efficiency lead to more focused activity, whereby '24/7' operations can by maintained from a single 'virtual' location. In the example of the global call-centre industry, an impression is deliberately created of social, cultural and geographic proximity to the customer. As employees work both day- and nightshifts, issues of time difference become irrelevant. Moreover, language skills are a basic requirement and a starting point for complex staff training aimed at the enforced change of accent, familiarization with elements of history and culture, and even the construction of false identities that encapsulate aspects of education and lived experience in the home country of the caller. UK companies routinely outsource customer service to Indian call centres in which staff has the language skills and technical knowledge to deal with inquiries, and receives regular updates of 'local knowledge' – the story line of soap operas, or the scores from the latest Premiership soccer matches – to enable them to engage in conversation with callers at a personal level.

Porter's fourth attribute – business strategy, structure and rivalry – relates to the organization's fit with, and flexibility in adapting to, prevailing business conditions in its home market over time. Porter highlights that there is no universal menu for business strategy. Rather, successful firms need to be willing and able to change in order to remain competitive within a dynamic business environment.

In addition to the above key attributes, Porter identifies two variables that have an impact upon them: chance and government-related factors. Chance encapsulates those major events or innovations that have not been foreseen and that have the capability of driving a fundamental reshaping of an industry. For example, the events of 11 September 2001 triggered immediate changes to the nature of the airline industry in the United States, and had wider impact at a global level in the months and years thereafter. As a less extreme example, the development of IT technologies and associated software has changed forever the nature of education. In many countries, academics are no longer afforded the opportunity to write a few notes on a blackboard, but must meet student expectations of providing presentations in an electronic format, and of uploading them on to online learning platforms.

The intervention of government in the nature of the business environment can come in a variety of forms. The most obvious examples include economic and legislative acts, ranging from changes in tax structures to subsidies offered to businesses in certain areas or, for example, country-specific legislation related to environmental protection. Governments also influence IB practice through their policy making. Government policies may relate directly to trade exchange, as, for example, in the elevation of some countries to the status of 'most favoured nations' (MFNs), whilst education policy can have an impact on the types and level of skills available in the workforce. At the extreme of government impact at a global level, legal constraints in developed economies coupled with an almost total lack of any form of protection for the environment or workforce in developing countries leads to the emergence of remarkable forms of international business. One such development is the shipbreaking industries of countries like Bangladesh, India and Pakistan (see Greenpeace, 2006). The breaking 'yards' of Chittagong in Bangladesh occupy some 20 kilometres of polluted beach on which the discarded super tankers and bulk carriers of the world are driven ashore at top speed then cut apart by a workforce of thousands, with no safety equipment and with no regard for the presence of asbestos, heavy metals and other toxic waste. Notwithstanding these concerns about safety and the environment, reports (Andersen, 2001) point to the fact that the steel from these hulks supplies 80% of Bangladesh's demand for reinforcing bars in the construction sector, material that this nation might not otherwise be able to afford.

critique of Porter's framework

Porter's model brings together elements of both country- and firm-based theories of international trade. As with earlier country-based theories, there is consideration of country-specific factor endowments and of their influence on trade flows. However, Porter places firms at the centre-stage of his framework and sees them as the key players in contemporary IB. The role of countries is seen by Porter as lying in the creation of an environment that either helps or hinders the extent to which firms are able to compete at an international level. At the same time, for Porter, the major driver of firm performance is the search for competitive advantage that will result in the generation of above-average profits and, hence, the highest return to financial shareholders. Any consideration of other factors is related to this in an instrumental way. Porter acknowledges that the possibilities for the global configuration of value-adding activities are underpinned by structural discrepancies across countries. These discrepancies may take the form of earning differentials between societies, as shown in the example we outlined above of the growth of EPZs, with recognition of the benefits firms can derive from countries offering low-cost labour as against those where labour costs are high. Variations in the cost of infrastructure provisions – buildings, roads, ports and power – provide further advantages to business. Also, differences in governmental regulatory frameworks, stipulating levels of tax and duty, environmental and labour laws, and degrees of intervention or *laissez-faire*, become central to decision making.

As we have highlighted, within Porter's analysis, economic, social, technological and legislative differentials between countries are seen as opportunities to be exploited in the search for competitive advantage, rather than as broader issues to be addressed at a global level. In an ever-more competitive global marketplace, this leads to firms consistently seeking to take advantage of developments in global supply chains and logistics in order to maximize the benefits accrued to shareholders, spreading their production networks into increasingly lower-waged economies. In mass-market consumer economies, this enables them to increase the range of product offerings, whilst constantly reducing the real cost of these to the consumer. For many in developed economies, this is seen as highly beneficial, not just in terms of company profits and shareholder wealth, but in allowing consumers to acquire more and more goods, many of which would previously have been beyond their purchasing power – or beyond their imagination and aspiration. However, in looking at the benefits accrued to us as consumers, those of us in the developed world are not always aware of the consequences of our consumption for those at the other end of the global supply chain.

In late 2006, in the run-up to Christmas shopping, the UK charity War on Want (2006) published a report that highlighted the plight of workers in the Bangladeshi garment industry that supplies three of the leading UK low-price fashion retailers. This document, widely reported in the media, outlined how wages in the industry in Bangladesh had halved, in real terms, during the 1990s as a result of companies' drive to reduce their production costs and their prices to consumers. According to War on Want, the basic wage provided to workers in 2006 did not meet the minimum necessary to cover living costs. The working time typically totalled 80 hours per week, with factories operating seven days a week. Conditions inside factories were described as unsafe and uncomfortable in the extreme, whilst working practices were subject to draconian control and, in the worst cases, underpinned by physical violence and deprivation of basic human rights. The legal working practices in Bangladesh do not match up to those that are seen in developed countries and, moreover, are frequently not subject to official control and enforcement of what regulations do exist. In addition, the local companies themselves are most often not part of the MNEs for which they operate, and therefore the multinationals can move their business freely between suppliers – between countries even – in order to maximize their own advantage.

Looking at the case of the Bangladeshi garment industry from the perspective of Porter's framework, the activities of the involved firms remain unproblematic, since it invokes no consideration of the ethical dimension of IB. Porter sees firms as operating within a given external environment, without obligation to influence it for the benefit of others. This approach accords with the maxim of the economist Milton Friedman (1962) to the effect that any business has but one social responsibility; to maximize the return on investment for its financial stakeholders through the most effective allocation of resources, as long as this is done fairly and competitively and within the legal frameworks that prevail. However Friedman himself recognized that this view of firms' responsibilities left unanswered the questions, 'Who protects the consumer?' and 'Who protects the worker?' (Friedman and Friedman, 1980). Whilst the first of these questions might open up a complex debate, the benefit to firms in seeking 'competitive advantage' by outsourcing production to countries where the second is not addressed is clear, as exemplified in 2006 when UK retailers had their best Christmas sales for three years.

critical engagement with the discourse of IB

The twentieth-century firm-based theories that we have discussed in this chapter constitute the major part of the canon of IB literature, and we have pointed to how the thinking that underpins them corresponds with the practices of MNEs. However, there are alternative discourses that challenge theoretical developments that focus on the generation of profit and shareholder value, without explicit consideration of impacts on broader society and with an implicit assumption that free markets will in the end benefit all. For example, there exists a body of social theories under the umbrella title 'dependency theory'. The roots of this critical response to mainstream economic theory lie in the work of the Economic Commission for Latin America (ECLA), starting in the 1950s and led by economist Raúl Prebisch (see Prebisch, 1971). The group's economic analysis identified a trend of deterioration in the terms of trade between Latin American countries and their richer trade partners in the north. This trend, they argued, commenced in the era of sixteenth-century colonialism and, over the centuries, resulted in a continuous decline in the wealth of poor nations as that of rich nations grew.

According to the theory, dependency is maintained through a series of mechanisms, ranging from political and economic policies, to exploitation of cheap natural and labour resources, cultural and intellectual hegemony, and the passing on of obsolete technologies. Moreover, dependency theorists point to the role of elites in the poor nations in maintaining the state of dependency and underdevelopment, through acting as enablers of – and being profiteers from – the activities of developed world MNEs and financial institutions. From its roots in Latin America, dependency theory spread and influenced scholars in the north, particularly neo-Marxists such as Andre Frank (1978). The relationship between rich and poor countries was also explored by Baran (1957), who considered the causes of some countries' 'underdevelopment' and linked these to the accumulation of the wealth derived from their natural and labour resources by the developed countries. Responses given by dependency theorists to the exploitative economic relationships they describe vary. Some, like Frank, do not see the possibility of escape within the capitalist system, whilst others, such as Cardoso (1972), consider that countries can seek to adjust the system to their benefit. Intellectually, dependency theory is drawn upon by authors from the 'world systems theory' school, to which we refer in Chapter 3.

conclusion

In this chapter, we have engaged with firm-based developments in trade theory and IB practice. We started from an overview of the changing nature of the IB environment from the mid-nineteenth century to the post-Second World War era, that underpins the shift in focus from country- to firm-based theories of IB. We then outlined key developments in these theories in the second half of the twentieth century, followed by a discussion of Porter's model of national competitive advantage. In particular, we have pointed to the centrality of the idea of profit maximization for MNEs within more recent theoretical frameworks of IB. Finally, by reference to dependency theory, we have offered an alternative view of the outcomes of IB activity for both developed and developing economies.

Following our exposition of theoretical developments in this chapter, we suggest that you might find it useful to consider the different answers to Flyvbjerg's four value-rational questions (see pages 6–7) that are invoked through analyzing the activities of contemporary MNEs by the application of them. For example, what is the impact of IB that takes place according to the principles of profit maximization and shareholder return upon the economies of developing countries? Are you, as a student of IB and as a citizen of the world, satisfied with the direction that this is taking? What, if anything, should be done about this? Is there anything you can do? Who are the winners and losers under the current rules of the game, and what exactly are the rules of the game?

3

Investment Theories of IB

This is why money is so called, because it exists not by nature but by custom, and it is in our power to change its value or render it useless.

Aristotle

▰▰▰▰ introduction

To this point, in discussing contemporary theories of trade, we have considered the movement of goods as influenced by factors of production and by firms' drive to profit-maximization through their exploitation. Neo-classical theories assumed the mobility of products and capital, and the immobility of labour. However, labour has been shown to have a degree of mobility across history. Examples of labour movement, which illustrate elements of both enforcement and choice, are the slave trade that saw millions of Africans transported to the New World and economic migration from Europe to other parts of the world in the nineteenth and twentieth centuries and, at the present time, to western Europe and the United States from developing and transition economy countries. Similarly, the assumption of capital mobility as a fundamental driver was to be challenged in the second half of the twentieth century in emergent 'investment theories' of IB. Alongside trade, international investments constitute the other major form of international business activity. The discussion that follows is centred first on the foreign direct investment approach to international investment. Thereafter, we address the issue of portfolio investment and the nature of contemporary global financial markets.

forms of international investment

The literature usually distinguishes between two main types of international investment, with the main criterion for the distinction being the question of control (see Hymer, 1960/1976). The first type, where foreign assets are acquired with the objective of taking control over them, is referred to as 'foreign direct investment' (FDI). In contrast to FDI – where control over operations in the host country is key – the second type of international investment is focused on a purely financial interest, without any drive for managerial control. This activity centres on purchases of shares, government bonds or other financial assets, and is classified as 'portfolio investment'. Contemporarily, portfolio investment takes place at the level of a global network of exchanges, for example, where pension funds seek to maximize the return on their members' investments by dealing in shares across the world's stock markets.

In addition to Hymer's two main types of investment, there are other ways of categorizing international capital transfer. Barbara Ingham (2004) outlines four categories. Other than FDI and portfolio investment, she lists 'bank loans' and 'official development flows'. The first of these relates to commercial lending by multinational banks, which may be directed either to companies or to governments. The second encapsulates finance offered to developing and transition economies, either by transnational agencies like the International Monetary Fund or World Bank, or by major donor countries such as Japan, France, the UK and the USA. Ingham points out that the last of these types of arrangement is often grounded in historical ties, or related to political, strategic or economic goals. For example, she highlights how France directs a substantial amount of its development finance to its former colonies in sub-Saharan Africa.

Ingham (2004) also differentiates between two major categories of international capital flow, namely equity and debt. With equity transfer, the home country investor takes some stake in the host country market, whether through FDI or portfolio investment. As such, the investor shares in the risk that the investment may either increase in value or depreciate. With debt investment, such as bonds and loans, however, the investor generally retains the original value of the capital transfer, plus interest due at the agreed rate. Except in the case of government default or institutional bankruptcy, the value of the investment is not related to the economic status of the host country or to the market value of the particular asset purchased with it.

In addition to the above types of investment, which involve capital transfer, Grazia Ietto-Gillies (2005) outlines a number of 'non-equity' investment types: licensing, franchising, alliances, and sub-contracting. We would refer readers to Ietto-Gillies' text for a detailed discussion of these different forms, beyond what we can cover here. However, these are also addressed in Dunning's (1980) 'eclectic theory' of international investment, which we will consider in this chapter.

foreign direct investment

In the past, FDI was mainly a one-way process, constituting one of the economic aspects of European imperialism and colonization of new territories. In the contemporary world, however, FDI investments take place at a global level within complex networks. For example, the global automotive industry has seen FDI from Japan and Europe to the United States, from Europe to Japan and Central America, from the USA to Europe and China, and from China, South Korea and Malaysia to Europe. FDI can be divided into a number of different sub-categories, based upon different criteria. One such categorization differentiates between 'greenfield' and 'merger and acquisition' (M&A) investments. Greenfield investment is centred on the setting up of a completely new operation in the host country, whereas M&A investment involves the home country firm in either joining with or purchasing an existing company in the host country.

Another classification of types of FDI introduces the distinction between 'horizontal FDI' and 'vertical FDI'. Horizontal FDI refers to activity whereby an organization invests in a business that operates in the same industry as itself. An example of horizontal FDI would be National Australia Bank's takeover of the UK Clydesdale Bank. In addition to being set in an intra-industry context, horizontal FDI has until recently taken place by and large between developed countries. However, contemporarily, examples are found of new players in the IB field from emerging economies participating in FDI in the developed economies, such as Indian Tata Steel's purchase of Anglo-Dutch Corus in the steel industry and Chinese Lenovo's acquisition of the PC division of IBM – the company that invented personal computers.

In contrast to horizontal FDI, vertical FDI may be inter-industry, whereby one organization seeks to procure sources of materials or components for its own products, or support services that underpin its market offerings. Vertical FDI will often be set in the context of developed-to-developing economy investment, whereby the home company often seeks to drive down the cost of doing business by exploiting lower-wage operations in the host country. An example of vertical FDI is the investment by UK service industries in call centres in India, which we discuss below, in order to deliver customer support on a lower cost basis than from the UK.

The distinction between horizontal and vertical FDI has important implications for the FDI recipient countries, and for the overall discussion about the benefits of FDI. In the hope of encouraging economic advancement, many developing countries initiate policies to attract FDI, with the expectation that this will result in increased employment and technological spillover. However, these positive effects are more likely to occur in the case of horizontal, rather than vertical, FDI. Since vertical FDI often involves locating the production of technologically simple and low-skilled labour-intensive elements in countries that are abundant in low-skilled labour, it has a much lower potential for generating spillovers and linkages. Based upon his empirical study of vertical

FDI in Mexico, Waldkirch (2003) concluded that its benefits in terms of job creation and economic contribution for the host country are limited. Despite the problematic nature of the effects of FDI on the host country economy, both horizontal and vertical FDI are considered as advantageous by MNEs and, with increasing globalization of the economy, the importance of FDI in the contemporary world has grown. For example, during the 1990s, world FDI flows grew by 535% compared to 85% increases in merchandise trade and 27% in world production (Waldkirch, 2003).

In proposing the first comprehensive theory of FDI, Steven Hymer (1960/1976) argued that the acquisition of assets in other countries does not necessarily require a transfer of capital, nor does it have to be driven by either prevailing financial or legal conditions, or by the desire to export finished products. In asserting that a move into a new market would not necessarily be based upon consideration of the 'favourable' conditions of that market, Hymer considered that such favourable conditions should first benefit home organizations, and that FDI adds costs and risks for the incoming firm. We do not have space to explain Hymer's reasoning in detail here, but would refer readers to his concepts of 'market imperfections' and 'conflict removal' as key drivers of FDI. The first refers to imbalances of factors of production and market structures between nations, whilst the second addresses the firm's desire to eliminate competition from its overall market.

Whatever form FDI takes, production is based in the host country without the transfer of goods from the home operation. At the same time, financing is frequently undertaken by borrowing within the host country and, as such, need not involve any transfer of capital between countries. In addition, profits generated within the host country may be reinvested there, rather than being transferred back to the home country. Hymer showed that FDI often builds into a complex set of relationships between nations that may involve a two-way flow of FDI, with no actual transfer of products or capital between them, and no reliance upon any overall advantageous economic or legal environment in one or other. Here, the FDI by both parties is entirely based upon borrowing within the respective host countries, delivery of the product or service within the host market, and reinvestment of profits generated also within the host nation.

Dunning's 'eclectic theory'

Broadening out from Hymer's FDI approach, further investment theories have been proposed. The most prolific writer on these is John Dunning (1977, 1980, 1993, 2000). Dunning developed a series of interpretations of drivers of the internationalization of business, identifying three sets of advantages that firms might seek to exploit, namely ownership, location and internalization (OLI). The first of these relates to a set of advantages that are specific to the firm, its competitive advantage over its rivals and its ability to exploit investment opportunities. Here, it is argued that a firm owning an asset that contributes to the creation of competitive advantage in the home market can exploit this advantage through entering foreign markets using FDI. Such assets may be either tangible or intangible, for example financial capital, technologies, skilled labour, natural resources, or intellectual capital. The second set is specific to a country: those structural features to attract inward investment. Location advantages may be derived, for example, from access to natural resources, the pool of available labour – whether manual or intellectual – or, as in the case of Singapore, from the country's position on global trade routes. The final set addresses why an organization might decide to internationalize through FDI rather than by other routes – for example, exporting, franchising or licensing. The internalization route is likely to be chosen by a firm where the transaction cost of pursuing one of these alternatives exceeds that of building its own international operations.

Whilst Dunning's 'eclectic theory' has been valuable because of its comprehensive treatment of a variety of factors governing foreign direct investment, critics point to its shortcomings in this very respect. Ietto-Gillies (2005) states what Dunning himself has acknowledged, that eclectic theory offers endless possibilities for examining motivations behind FDI, such that it can always be applied as an explanatory framework without fear of falsification. Beyond this critique at a theoretical level, we would point to issues in contemporary IB practice that run counter to Dunning's propositions. Whilst Dunning identifies advantages in ownership and internalization, the 1980s and 1990s saw many MNEs seeking to build competitive advantage through processes of outsourcing and contracting. In the examples of fashion garment production given by War on Want (referred to in Chapter 2), the organizations prioritized production flexibility and the ability to source at the lowest possible cost over building longer-term embeddedness through ownership or internalization.

In the services sector, similar differences in location based upon strategic considerations can be identified. In the UK banking and building society sector, some organizations have outsourced to low-wage economies, others have maintained their UK operations, and there is evidence that yet others have used the 'offshoring' approach and have subsequently retrenched operations into the home country. In 2003, Norwich Union became one of the major outsourcers of service centre jobs to India, citing reasons of increased flexibility, capacity, efficiency and improved customer service. In 2007, in what commentators described as a 'dramatic U-turn' (Foxwell, 2007a), the organization announced that it was moving call-centre work back to the UK, following negative customer reaction to service levels provided from the outsourced operations. The power company Powergen adopted a similar policy of repatriation of its service operations in 2006 (Foxwell, 2007a).

In addition to the possibility of identifying the shortcomings of Dunning's approach by pointing to examples from IB practice, a major problem with it, from our perspective, is that it addresses the topic of investment entirely from the investing company's point of view. Where it speaks about 'advantages' or 'costs', the advantages and costs considered relate to the internationalizing firm. At the same time, the theory is silent about what FDI does to local companies, to the natural environment, or to the communities affected in terms of the amount of employment created or tax revenues generated for the host country. By contrast, as we have pointed out above, FDI is not necessarily advantageous for the host country and, as empirical examples suggest, it may result in driving local companies out of business, polluting the natural environment and depleting local natural resources, whilst generating few employment opportunities for local people and little or no tax revenue for the host government. As we discuss in Chapter 7, contemporary MNEs may use a range of tax strategies in order to minimize their global tax liability. We would argue for the need to approach the subject of FDI from the perspective of all affected parties and Dunning's theory, despite its acclaimed comprehensiveness, has not been applied to this end.

knowledge-capital model of FDI

Another theoretical framework that addresses the determinants of FDI location is Markusen's (1998) 'knowledge-capital' (KK) model. He incorporates consideration of the distinction between horizontal and vertical FDI into this model in order to explain how domestic firms as well as vertically- or horizontally-integrated MNEs develop. Markusen's model is based upon three major assumed conditions, which he terms fragmentation, skilled-labour intensity and jointness. The first of these implies the possibility for the location of knowledge-based assets to be fragmented from those of production. Here, it is assumed that the incremental cost of knowledge transfer to a foreign plant is small, relative to that of supplying a single domestic plant. The second condition is that the generation of these knowledge services is more skilled-labour intensive than is the production element. Finally, the notion of jointness relates to the ability to share knowledge-based assets across multiple production locations. It is important to distinguish between the first and third of these assumptions. An example of fragmentation is where a multinational oil company has a small team of seismographers based, say, in its home at Houston, Texas. It is more effective for the company to send the team to operate in different locations as required than to provide this specialist service across all individual country operations. However, the seismographic team can only operate in one location at any one time. In comparison, an example of jointness is seen where the modern car manufacturing group, such as Ford or General Motors, centralizes its design expertise for platforms, engines, gearboxes, etc. in particular locations, but can share the knowledge output from these across the world simultaneously.

According to the KK model, the implications of the existence of fragmentation and skilled-labour intensity are such that MNEs will engage in vertical FDI in different countries, depending upon factor prices and market sizes. On the other hand, the occurrence of jointness will give rise to MNEs investing horizontally, that is, producing final goods in a number of countries. In other words, Markusen's model links the emergence of vertical and horizontal FDI by MNEs to differences in country characteristics, such as size, factor endowments, costs of trade and investment costs.

Within the KK model, as with other theories and models discussed thus far, there is an unstated assumption that the firm is the central actor in international investment, having agency to construct its global structures depending upon the various factors outlined above. As such, it is again seen as unproblematic that MNEs' exploitation of structural differences between countries for the benefit of their own production and process efficiency and profit maximization is likely to be at the expense of resource exploitation and depletion, environmental degradation and increasing socio-economic fragmentation.

portfolio investment

Whilst FDI has been the central focus of much discussion of international investment, as outlined at the start of this chapter, it is not necessary that the key objective of such investment will be ownership of or control over a company or any physical asset. Portfolio investment is directed towards the acquisition of 'paper assets' in another country. These may take the form of, for example, equities or bonds. The first of these, which might involve a shareholding in a foreign company without control or ownership, falls within Ingham's (2004) category of equity investment, whereby the investor shares in the risk that the value of the investment may fall, rather than increasing. The second type is a form of debt transfer, whereby the face value of the bond (i.e. of the initial capital investment in whatever agreed currency) is maintained and interest is due on the investment. As explained above, except in circumstances of default by or bankruptcy of the bond issuer, the bond holder carries no share of risks.

The importance of portfolio investments increased greatly in the early 1990s, with the easing of international exchange controls and growth in the amount of developed country capital seeking high rates of return at a time of low interest rates in the home economies. During this time, cross-border capital flows grew to exceed the amount of international trade flows. That is to say, 'paper investments' became more important than those in 'real' entities, such as companies or physical assets. For a period, the world economy supported growth and return on portfolio investments, largely through the rapid development of the economies of South East Asia and Russia, with their thirst for goods and services in their home markets and their strong export performance to developed economies. This prompted an influx of external capital from investors seeking above average returns on the capital invested. However, the growth rate proved unsustainable as, first, the Japanese domestic market slowed down and confidence in other economies, particularly Thailand, faltered. Thailand had been a net importer of capital in the early 1990s, largely through portfolio investment rather than FDI, and as such the capital could be withdrawn with relative ease as the country's currency started to lose value. The 'Asian financial crisis' that followed on from the collapse of the Thai economy had repercussions across the world's financial markets, illustrating the interconnectedness and dependency of country economies at a global level. As we reach the conclusion of this writing project in January 2008, the complexity, opaqueness and all-embracing impact of global portfolio investment flows is witnessed as the impacts of the US sub-prime mortgage crisis spread across the world's financial institutions and economies.

beyond the centrality of nations and the 'firm'

If we reflect upon the foundations of extant investment theories, we might wish to challenge their implicit assumptions about the purpose of IB, and to take account of alternative socio-political and environmental perspectives. Mainstream writers on FDI base their ideas upon the notion that the capitalist firm is the main actor in IB, and that it legitimately seeks to maximize its profits by achieving production efficiency through FDI. This view is in line with those that underpin classical theories of international trade, as first put forward by Smith, Torrens and Ricardo. These theories, as explained in Chapter 1, proposed that countries should specialize in the production of those goods that they are able to manufacture most efficiently. Viewed from this perspective, contemporary FDI – through the activities of MNEs – can be considered as contributing to the attainment of the most efficient distribution and configuration of production at a global level. It is this rationale that is adopted by those who justify the current processes of globalization of industries. However, Smith's and others' argumentation was firmly rooted in the concept of a free market and in the belief that such a free market would ultimately lead to the accumulation of wealth for all nations, to the benefit of all citizens relative to their own previous situation.

The assumptions that underpin these theories are problematic in a number of ways. At a theoretical level, they can be challenged by Marxist political and economic theory which, rather than viewing MNEs as facilitators of wealth generation for all, sees them as instruments of exploitation and appropriation of resources to the sole benefit of their home country shareholders. As Glyn (2006) points out, the enhanced potential for mobility of location for firms from rich countries inherent in FDI under free market economic conditions leads to a weakened position for workers in the home country in wage or employment negotiations. Similarly, it puts workers in the host country in a situation of uncertainty of employment, stemming from the possibility that the foreign investment may be withdrawn.

Whilst the analysis of world trade offered by dependency theory, referred to in Chapter 2, distinguishes between 'core' and 'periphery', 'world systems theory' (see Wallerstein, 1974, 2004) argues that the global economic system is characterized by a division of labour between three zones: core, semi-periphery and periphery. In this model, which is defined in terms of power relations – political, economic and military – the nations at the core are those that exercise dominance over others, but are not themselves dominated. Those at the periphery, on the other hand, are subject to domination, but hold no power over others. The middle category consists of those countries that are both exploiters of others, at the periphery, but are themselves exploited by the core. Whilst they benefit from their exploitation through accruing some of the benefits of world economic activity, they lack military might that would allow them to take control over redistribution of economic output. This group is seen as essential for the smooth operation of the world capitalist system, which otherwise would be polarized and, hence, less politically stable.

As far as specific types of economic activity within the world system are concerned, companies from the core and the semi-periphery are in a privileged position compared to those at the periphery. With the support of their home governments, they are able to secure control over the most profitable activities within the international division of labour, generating high profits for themselves and contributing to the perpetuation of a situation of inequality. Within a hierarchical ordering, the countries of the core maintain their control over the semi-periphery, and the semi-periphery over periphery. Viewed through the lens of world systems theory, FDI is seen by some as not constituting a politically neutral activity of a purely economic nature. Rather, it is considered as an instrument of control used by powerful nations to dominate the less powerful ones.

The political dimension of FDI is also evident when discussion of foreign investment and its impacts takes place from a neo-colonial perspective. Through adopting this approach, it can be argued that MNEs and the institutions of FDI have a vested interest in perpetuating historical differences in levels of economic, social and technological development in order to maintain the home country entities' domination over host country factors of production. As some commentators point out, these types of activity by MNEs, governments and other IB actors are symptomatic of an inherent problem of IB: that it is and always will be dominated by powerful actors who will dictate the rules of the game and what constitutes freedom within it.

conclusion to Part I

In the first three chapters of this book, we have sought to present the historical antecedents of IB and outline the development of theories that underpin it. In doing this, we have aimed to offer an understanding of how thinking about IB as both an intellectual and a practical domain has, throughout centuries, been rooted in specific political, economic, social and technological contexts. We have attempted to convey to you that the particular way in which IB has evolved, as well as its current status has not been a purely 'natural' process, in the sense of having been determined by market forces operating under the conditions of perfect competition. Rather, it has been influenced by certain actors in pursuit of their interests at different points in time. It has also been strongly connected to the development of capitalism as the prevalent economic system in Europe, and to its spread across the world.

In the case of earlier developments in IB, these powerful political and economic actors were nation states, whilst the twentieth century saw the emergence of MNEs as the most powerful entities engaging in IB practices. We have discussed how the rise of these entities was accompanied by theoretical developments that placed firms centre-stage and addressed questions of how they compete internationally or globally, and how they can maximize their profits, and hence, shareholder return.

We have pointed to how theoretical underpinnings of IB are rooted in the assumption that international exchange is an inherently 'good' project, as it leads to wealth creation, improvements in efficiency and increasing consumption. Whilst you will have your own views on what is 'good' and what is 'bad' about IB, we have attempted to provoke critical reflection on issues of loss and transfer of jobs at a global level, increasing economic inequalities between and within nations, and exploitative work conditions in low-cost locations, as well as on resource depletion, environmental degradation and climate change. In addition, we have introduced alternative theoretical frameworks to those of the IB canon that can support a more detailed critical analysis of these issues. In the meantime, we suggest a starting point for engagement via contemplation of extant theories and practices using Flyvbjerg's (2001) four value-rational questions:

- Where are we going?
- Is this development desirable?
- What, if anything, should we do about it?
- Who gains and who loses, and by which mechanisms of power?

In Part II, we will move on to consider a variety of actors shaping and impacted by contemporary IB practices and the interdependencies between them.

Part 11

Actors in International Business

4

Institutions of International Business

■■■ introduction

In Part I, we presented an overview of international business as both a theoretical and practical domain from an historical perspective. In particular, we drew attention to the shift in focus of international trade and IB from being country- to firm-based. Here, we discuss the contemporary institutional frameworks underpinning IB and, in so doing, outline the various factors that contributed to their emergence and development over time. An awareness of at least some aspects of the political and economic conditions that prevailed at different times in the nineteenth and twentieth centuries is essential for an understanding of the present role and status of key institutions like the International Monetary Fund (IMF), the World Bank and the World Trade Organization (WTO). It is also helpful in comprehending the growth of new structures of economic cooperation and integration between countries, such as the Association of South East Asian Nations (ASEAN) and the Common Market of the South (MERCOSUR). In engaging with various views regarding the implications of these institutions for different actors, we develop a discussion in which they are seen as being both key to the solution and part of the problem of trade imbalance and economic inequalities at a global level. In problematizing the role of government-sponsored institutional frameworks, we consider the role and impact of a range of social movements and non-governmental organizations (NGOs) that act as loci of resistance, and we point to the theoretical possibilities for an alternative global order.

the international monetary system

Since ancient times, trade that was not based upon barter (i.e. exchange of goods) has been most frequently undertaken using gold coins as the means of payment. However, with the development and growth of international trade from the nineteenth century on, it became impractical to use gold as the payment medium as, for example, in transporting a shipload of gold from London to Hong Kong in order to pay for a consignment of China tea. In order to move to a system of currency-based trade exchange, between 1870 and 1914 the main players in international trade adopted a 'gold standard' system, whereby the value of their individual currencies was 'pegged' to that of gold. In this way, each currency had a defined conversion rate in relation to the weight of gold for which it could be exchanged and, thereby, countries could value their own currency in relation to any other using this common yardstick. The emergence of the gold standard was paralleled by the economic and colonial domination of the United Kingdom, in an era when it was said that 'the sun never sets on the British Empire'. During this period, the pound sterling was the strongest and most widely used currency in settling international transactions and, not surprisingly, London emerged as the major financial centre in the world.

With the outbreak of the First World War, countries withdrew from the gold standard and, despite efforts to reinstate it in the interwar years, it finally collapsed with the economic downturn of the Great Depression that began in October 1929, as countries became more preoccupied with their internal economic problems than with supporting free international trade. In 1931, the Bank of England cut the link between the value of gold and that of sterling, allowing the pound to 'float' on international financial exchanges with its value determined by market forces. Until the outbreak of the Second World War, the lack of stability within the international monetary system had not been resolved. Towards the end of the war, at the Bretton Woods conference of 1944, which was intended to provide a framework for global economic and social stability, one of the agreements reached was that the US dollar would be tied to the value of gold, and all other countries would peg their currencies to the dollar. Individual countries retained freedom to apply controls to the flow of private capital and they could only seek a revaluation of their currency where they found themselves in conditions of 'fundamental disequilibrium'.

The Bretton Woods system combined the objectives of trade liberalization with governments' desire to maintain degrees of control over their domestic economies. However, its lifespan was limited to less than thirty years and a number of factors contributed to its failure. First, from the 1950s, in parallel with the dollar-bound currency exchange system, 'euromarkets' emerged as a major attractor of foreign currency deposits in European banks. This Eurocurrency market was not subject to government capital controls and, as such, it grew rapidly, contributing to the increasing strength of European economies. On the other hand, throughout the 1960s, the US economy experienced rising inflation and a growing trade deficit. Also in the 1960s, members of the Organization of the Petroleum Exporting Countries (OPEC) started to exercise their economic power, significantly raising the price of oil and generating high levels of earnings that they subsequently invested in international money markets. The growing complexity of international financial flows, coupled with economic uncertainty around the world, led to a questioning of the ability of the signatories of the Bretton Woods agreement to fulfil their commitments. In 1971, the system finally collapsed when US President Richard Nixon announced the end of convertibility of the US dollar to gold.

A new framework establishing the rules governing the international monetary system was settled in January 1976, known as the Jamaica Agreement. The agreement stipulated that the value of world currencies would not be fixed, but that countries would be allowed to choose the exchange system that would be most suitable to their economic interests. Some countries chose to allow their currency to float in relation to others, whilst others decided to peg theirs to that of another country. The examples of Hong Kong and the European Economic Community (EEC) are illustrative of the diversity of adopted solutions. Hong Kong has pegged the value of its dollar to that of the US dollar for over twenty years, maintaining this link beyond its transition from being a British colony to becoming a Special Administrative Region (SAR) of the People's Republic of China (PRC). As part of the European integration process, which we discuss later in this chapter, members of the EEC created the European Monetary System (EMS), within which most countries joined the 'exchange rate mechanism' (ERM). Under the ERM, individual currency exchange rates were fixed against one another within a range of +/- 2.25% of par value, whilst maintaining a floating rate in relation to the US dollar and to other non-ERM currencies. The establishment of the EMS facilitated the introduction of the euro by a number of European countries, first as an accounting currency in 1999, then in the form of banknotes and coins in 2002. Whilst, within the contemporary international monetary system both pegged and fixed exchange rate mechanisms are adopted, a number of leading economies, including the USA and Japan, employ an approach that permits their currency to float according to market forces, at the same time allowing space for government intervention. This takes place through setting interest rates, taxation regimes and other domestic financial frameworks in order to influence the economic environment. However, many would argue that the international financial system is now so complex that individual countries have only limited influence over their currency's value on the exchanges.

origins of the International Monetary Fund

As well as setting the post-Second World War international monetary system framework, the Bretton Woods conference also saw the establishment of two of the supranational institutions that play a key role in the contemporary world of IB: the International Monetary Fund and the International Bank for Reconstruction and Development (IBRD), now commonly referred to as the World Bank. The underlying objective behind the creation of these two bodies was, in the words of the then US Treasury Secretary Henry Morgenthau, the 'creation of a dynamic world community in which the peoples of every nation will be able to realise their potentialities' (Bretton Woods Project, 2005). The IMF has grown from an original membership of less than 50 countries in 1945 to 185 nations at present. The stated purpose of the IMF is to facilitate international monetary exchange and enable orderly exchange arrangements, to foster conditions of exchange stability, and to promote economic growth and high levels of employment at a global level. In addition, the IMF's task is to provide temporary financial support to countries that experience balance of trade and currency exchange difficulties. Financial assistance from the IMF is conditional upon the implementation of economic reforms that are designed to enable countries to address their balance of payments problems. The IMF stipulates specific structural adjustment policies for its borrowers and loans are issued in instalments only as these are put in place.

The IMF operates in three areas. First, it undertakes surveillance, monitoring economic and financial developments and providing policy advice specifically aimed at crisis prevention. Second, it lends to countries experiencing balance of payments difficulties in order to provide temporary finance and, additionally, to offer policies aimed at correcting the underlying problems. According to the IMF, loans to poorer countries are specifically directed towards poverty reduction. Third, the IMF offers technical assistance to countries to provide training in its areas of expertise. In support of these three areas, the IMF undertakes research and gathers economic statistics. More recently, aiming to strengthen the international financial system and to increase its effectiveness at preventing and resolving crises, the IMF has worked towards both developing standards and codes of good practice in its areas of responsibility and strengthening financial sectors globally.

The IMF gains most of its funding from its members' 'quota subscriptions', the amounts of which are based upon the relative size of their economies. The size of the quota also determines the extent to which the individual member country can draw upon IMF support when required. More significantly, voting rights within the IMF are determined by the relative size of the quota and, as such, the USA is the largest subscriber and holds the biggest bloc of votes.

growth and development of the World Bank

The largest public development institution in the world, the World Bank is based in Washington, DC and has 185 member countries, with participation being contingent upon membership of the IMF. It was established with the purposes of 'assist(ing) in the reconstruction and development of territories of members by facilitating the investment of capital for productive purposes' and of 'promot[ing] the long-range balanced growth of international trade and the maintenance of equilibrium in balances of payments by encouraging international investment ... thereby assisting in raising the productivity, the standard of living and conditions of labour in their territories' (World Bank, 1989, articles of agreement). The World Bank (2007) presents itself as 'a vital source of financial and technical assistance to developing countries around the world'. The term 'World Bank' is commonly used in joint reference to two specific institutions: the original IBRD, which was reconstituted as the lending arm of the bank to 'middle-income' countries (MICs), and the International Development Association (IDA), founded in 1960, which offers funds to the world's poorest nations.

Altogether, five institutions form what is referred to as the World Bank Group, namely, the original International Bank for Reconstruction and Development (IBRD), the International Development Association (IDA), the International Finance

Corporation (IFC), the Multilateral Investment Guarantee Agency (MIGA), and the International Centre for Settlement of Investment Disputes (ICSID). In addition to the IBRD and IDA, the IFC offers loan and equity finance for private sector projects in developing countries, whilst the role of the MIGA is to support foreign direct investment to developing countries through providing political risk insurance. The function of the ICSID is to facilitate settlement of disputes between member governments and foreign investors in investment-related matters. The administration of the World Bank encompasses all of these five institutions, with a common Board of Governors led by the World Bank president, who is appointed by the US government. In order to obtain necessary loan funds, the Bank issues bonds and sells them on international capital markets. To ensure that the loans are repaid, the Bank (like the IMF) imposes conditions upon borrowing countries, typically involving social, structural and sectoral reforms. As with the IMF, the extent of the influence of an individual member country upon the World Bank's decision-making processes depends upon the amount of the member's capital subscription. As such, the USA holds 20% of the voting rights and has its own Executive Director, in comparison with 7% and two Executive Directors shared amongst the 47 sub-Sahara African countries.

critiques of the IMF and the World Bank

As outlined above, the decision-making processes and voting rights within the IMF and World Bank are heavily influenced by individual member countries' financial contribution, which is determined by the size of their economies. As such, the major locus of power lies within the leading industrialized countries, specifically the G8 group of nations, which comprises Canada, France, Germany, Italy, Japan, Russia, the UK and the USA. Together, these countries control around 65% of the global economy and the majority of military resources. They are thereby in a position to formulate policies with little consultation with less developed nations. Critics point to how these policies do not necessarily result in improvements to the social and economic conditions for those countries that are the subject of IMF and World Bank programmes. On the contrary, IMF policies have been seen as leading to a reduction in public access to basic services, an increase in the incidence of poverty and to economic contraction and recession. This is seen as stemming from the 'structural adjustment' terms upon which support is conditional. It has been highlighted that, in many cases, these terms (often described as grounded in the neo-liberal 'Washington consensus') emphasize the need for the liberalization of trade and investment in the country's financial sector as well as the privatization and deregulation of state-owned enterprises (SOEs). Since recipient country governments are obliged to comply with the requirements of the IMF or World Bank structural adjustment programmes, criticisms have been expressed regarding the lack of consideration of local circumstances and, in addition, the potential removal of a country's ability to shape its own economic policies.

In relation to the World Bank, concerns have been expressed about the social and environmental consequences of some of the major infrastructure projects that it has supported. It has been attacked, in particular, for its support for hydroelectric dam projects in developing countries, where critics say that the social and environmental impacts on local inhabitants and habitats outweigh the benefits to the countries. In 2005, the Bank agreed to provide loans and guarantees worth $1.2 billion for a hydroelectric scheme in Laos, designed to earn foreign currency from electricity exports to neighbouring Thailand, despite claims that it would damage the environment and the livelihood of thousands of local villagers (Montlake, 2005). Stung by criticisms of its involvement in such developments, the Bank did decide not to offer funding for China's controversial Three Gorges Dam project. This decision did not, however, influence European, Japanese and Canadian governments, which provided support and finance for their domestic lenders and suppliers to the project. This scheme, the world's largest hydroelectric power development on the Yangtze River, was criticized from the outset by environmentalists, who described it as an inevitable ecological disaster, a prophetic view that even the Chinese government now echoes (Macartney, 2007).

The World Bank has also been criticized for its involvement in private sector investment in developing countries, especially where it has offered support for the delivery of healthcare and education by private providers who may supplant the country's own public sector provision. In the field of healthcare, the Bank's 2002 Private Sector Development (PSD) strategy was attacked by a broad range of NGOs (see Yamey, 2001) and civil society groupings, which considered that, despite its stated aim of ensuring that 'our dream is a world free of poverty', the World Bank's support for private hospital development in countries like India would benefit only the rich and increase social divisions.

As the IMF and World Bank constitute major international players, not only in the field of development finance and the setting of its regulatory frameworks, but also in research, training and publishing, critics express concern about their status as the perceived 'experts' in the area, and the resultant subordination or elimination of alternative discourses that challenge the neo-liberal view of development that they expound.

international trade regulation

In addition to setting the framework for the establishment of the IMF and World Bank, the initial Bretton Woods agreement incorporated a plan for the creation of an International Trade Organization (ITO). Whilst these plans were not fulfilled until 1995 with the setting up of the World Trade Organization (WTO), the Bretton Woods conference laid the ground for a series of meetings on trade regulation under the auspices of the United Nations. These meetings led to the establishment of the General Agreement on Tariffs and Trade (GATT) which, from 1948 until 1994, constituted the rules for a substantial amount of world trade during a period of unprecedented growth in international trade. Despite its development across various rounds of negotiation, GATT was never formalized as a set of binding conditions to which all countries signed up. During periods of economic turmoil in the 1970s and 1980s, accompanied by a resurgence of protectionist policies by national governments, it became apparent that the outcomes of the GATT negotiations were not effective, being insufficient to address the complexities of contemporary international trade and relations. In 1993, the GATT was revised and further obligations were placed upon signatories. However, the most significant development in this round of negotiations was the agreement that led to the setting up of the World Trade Organization. The WTO was established at the outset as an institutional body that brought together the existing 75 GATT members and those of the European Community.

the World Trade Organization

The main functions of the Geneva-based WTO, which has grown to 150 member countries, now include administering trade agreements, constituting a forum for trade negotiations between member countries, handling trade disputes, monitoring national trade policies, providing technical assistance and training for developing countries, and engaging in cooperation with other international organizations. Whilst the main objective of the WTO is the liberalization of world trade, its declared priorities also include ensuring the protection of consumer rights, supporting prevention of the spread of disease, and enhancing protection of the environment. The system of multilateral agreements within the WTO covers trade in goods, services and intellectual property rights.

The key principles set out by the WTO stipulate that member countries should engage in trade with each other without discrimination and should not give preferential treatment to their domestic products and services. These principles are encapsulated within the concept of 'most favoured nation' (MFN), whereby countries which grant this status to one another commit themselves to extending any preferential tariffs that they negotiate with one member state to all other members. In addition, the MFN principle implies that imported goods from other member states, along with services provided and copyrights and patents held by their organizations, will be subject to the same treatment as domestic products, services and intellectual properties. WTO members are obliged to engage in negotiation to remove barriers to trade, and to commit to and be bound by the outcomes of these negotiations. Furthermore, WTO principles discourage practices which are seen as being 'unfair', such as the provision of export subsidies and the 'dumping' of products at below-cost. In the period from the 1940s to the present, the GATT and WTO have brought about reductions in tariffs on international trade from an average of 40% to around 4%.

Within the terms of general WTO membership, some exceptions to the rules are allowed. First, countries are permitted to establish free trade agreements that apply only to goods traded within WTO member states, thus discriminating against goods from non-members. On the other hand, they can grant special access to their markets to developing countries. In addition, where one country considers that another is trading its goods unfairly, it can raise barriers against products from that country. In relation to services, countries are allowed to discriminate in favour of domestic suppliers, but in limited circumstances. Overall, WTO rules permit such exceptions only under strict conditions. Notwithstanding the key tenet of equality of treatment, the WTO does hold to a principle that confers beneficial status to less developed countries (LDCs), in allowing them additional time, flexibility and preferential terms for adjustment to WTO accession.

critiques of the WTO

As outlined above, the WTO concentrates its efforts on the liberalization of trade, according to the belief that free trade is good for all countries, including the poorest ones, as it is supposed to lead to their development. However, critics see problems with this ideological stance of neo-liberal economics. They point to empirical evidence which shows that free trade does not necessarily lead to development and economic growth. In particular, they argue that trade liberalization has not benefited developing countries. One

example of how it can have a negative effect was seen when prices
paid to Mexican farmers for maize halved when Mexico opened
its market to cheap US maize exports. In recent years, the USA
has been criticized by many for its continuing subsidization of agriculture, leading one North African ambassador at the WTO to
comment that 'The message from North to South in the Uruguay
Round was "you continue to liberalise we'll continue to subsidise"'
(Green, no date).

Academics in the field of environmental studies problematize
the key underlying assumption that economic development is
good for all nations, and that it should be prioritized over other
policy objectives. They point to how the drive to economic growth
is dependent upon material improvement through increased gross
domestic product (GDP) and that this requires increasing
exploitation of finite natural resources. The resultant resource
depletion leads to losses of natural habitats and of species, and to
increasing levels of environmental pollution and global warming.
Similarly, human rights groups and trade union movements argue
that the WTO does not take sufficient cognizance of issues of
child labour, forced labour and other forms of exploitation. In
this context, the WTO is criticized for not engaging with social
and environmental issues in a meaningful way.

Whilst proponents of the WTO point to the fact that, unlike other
transnational agencies such as the International Labour Organization
(ILO), it has the power to impose sanctions on member states who
transgress its rules, critics highlight that these powers can be fairly
limited. For example, they question whether the leave given to
Ecuador to impose sanctions on European Union (EU) member
states in a dispute over bananas provided any effective power to
the country, since the relative size and power of the economies of
Ecuador and the European Union meant that any ban would have
little impact upon the EU's economic situation. Additionally, since
the WTO does not issue any loans or provide funding for projects,
it cannot apply any punitive financial sanctions through withhold-
ing monies. It has also been pointed out that, as developed world
governments and transnational firms prove adept at manipulating

and applying WTO rules for their own benefit, they deprive developing countries of export opportunities which far exceed the value of the total aid funding provided to them. It is further highlighted that rules of 'equality' of trade are applied in a global marketplace that is already moulded by the inequalities of the past, as outlined in Part I. Here, the new rules of the game do not provide a level playing field but, rather, prevent developing nations from benefiting their nascent industries by application of the very protectionist policies that enabled the developed countries to achieve their current global dominance.

economic integration

In addition to those agencies, such as the IMF, World Bank and WTO, that are designed to operate globally at a supranational level, the period since the Second World War has seen steady development of a range of regional trade agreements and other forms of localized economic integration in different parts of the world. Many of these have not been established for purely economic reasons, such as the removal of trade barriers between members, but to serve also as loci of regional and geopolitical power. There exists a variety of forms and degrees of economic integration, as conceptualized by Balassa (1962). These include: the free trade area (FTA), customs union, common market, economic union and political union.

The first category refers to a situation where member countries agree to remove barriers to trade within their trading bloc, yet maintain separate trade policies in relation to non-member states. One example of an FTA is the North American Free Trade Agreement (NAFTA) which comprises Canada, Mexico and the United States. In the case of a customs union, members not only adopt a free trade policy amongst themselves, but they also agree a common trade policy framework for their individual dealings with other countries. At the present time, we identify no remaining grouping that falls into this category, but in the nineteenth century various principalities that now comprise modern Germany set up such a union, the *Zollverein*.

A common market assumes not only a customs union, but also a free movement of goods, labour and capital within its borders. Here, both workers and firms are free to relocate, in theory at least, in order to exploit the most advantageous conditions within particular member states. A contemporary example of the common market is MERCOSUR, the grouping of Argentina, Brazil, Paraguay and Uruguay. The fourth step in economic integration is economic union, whereby, in addition to the conditions of a common market, all economic policies, including monetary, fiscal and welfare policies, are set collectively by members. At present, the European Union is seen as the closest empirical example of economic union, with an aim for further economic and political integration. At the time of writing, the EU consists of 27 members and constitutes a single market that embraces a number of common policies on trade, agriculture and fisheries, and regional development. Moreover, 13 of the member states have thus far adopted the single European currency, the euro. In addition, the EU incorporates a number of bodies such as the European Commission, the Council of the European Union, the European Council, the European Central Bank, the European Court of Justice, and the European Parliament. Despite this high level of integration, to date, EU countries still pursue largely individual foreign policies and administer separate internal judicial and security policies.

Political union itself represents total integration of two or more countries into one, whereby each vests political and economic sovereignty in the new nation and relinquishes all national institutions. The reunification of East and West Germany in 1990 provides an example of the establishment of such a political union. Whilst, for some, the notion of full political union in Europe is a desired future state, at present, there remains strong opposition to this in many quarters.

critiques of economic integration

Extant examples of economic blocs and other types of integration show various forms of regionalization, whereby economic cooperation and interdependence increase within specific geographic areas. Proponents of this trend point to its positive outcomes for the involved countries in terms of expansion of markets and over-all economic growth. Critics, however, emphasize how the bene-fits of economic integration are often not distributed equally amongst all parties. For example, in the case of NAFTA, it is pointed out that US firms are able to set up operations in Mexico in order to exploit a pool of cheap labour and less constraining operating conditions. At the same time, however, the USA main-tains and currently aims to reinforce controls on immigration by Mexicans who seek to take advantage of employment and busi-ness opportunities in the United States. As Mexican markets have opened up for American companies, so the Mexican economy has become more and more dependent upon and tied to that of its powerful neighbour. This, some argue, has led to a reduction in Mexico's chances of competing effectively in the international economic arena on its own terms. They highlight that much of the country's export earnings, along with employment opportunities for its workforce, is tied to production by US (plus Japanese and EU) firms located in the *maquiladoras*, the export processing zones (EPZs) that enable them to operate largely outside Mexican taxa-tion and import/export duty frameworks.

Critical voices have also been raised in relation to the espoused and actual benefits of membership of the European Union. Whilst it is acknowledged that the EU has provided a platform for greater political and social stability in post-Second World War Europe, some point out that, in its current form, it does not offer equal advantages for all its members. The Union was initially built on principles of free movement of goods, ser-vices, capital and people and the realization of these was the case for early entrants. However, in relation to the accession countries which joined in 2004 and 2006, there have been selective limits applied by various existing members, for example, on the move-ment of workers. Overall, whilst some see regional economic inte-gration as providing benefits in expanding markets and opportunities, others consider it as reinforcing economic and political domination by the already powerful nations within any given bloc. Moreover, critics point out that this integration takes place largely around the imperative of economic growth and, thereby, other objectives, including those of a social and environmental nature, are subjugated to this end.

▓▓▓▓ global political economy, poverty and inequality

As outlined above, post-Second World War developments in global political economy have had impacts on the conditions in which IB transactions take place and on the economic situation of societies worldwide. Commenting on the trends observable in relation to the distribution of wealth between countries, Milanovic (2005) points to two phenomena: the 'Africanization' of poverty and the 'Westernization' of wealth. He highlights how, over time, the position of Africa, as well as Latin America and the Carribbean (LAC) has deteriorated. He also shows how, in the period between 1960 and 2000, the number of countries within the 'Fourth World' – that is, those countries whose GDPs are less than a third of the GDP per capita of the poorest western country – has increased from 25 to almost three times as many. At present, in almost all regions of the world, with the exception of the west, belonging to the category of the poorest countries is the most common condition, with 80% of African countries, and between 50% and 60% of countries in other regions currently being part of the Fourth World.

So why has the existence of institutions aiming at the opening-up of economies and the creation of conditions for growth for all not led to the poorer countries catching up with the rich? The answer to this question is partly found in the trajectory along which the rules of trade have evolved, to the advantage of the developed nations and the detriment of the developing world. This has been characterized by a strict approach in relation to those aspects of trade in which rich countries win in competition with the poor, and by the application of protectionist measures with regard to those in which the rich do not have competitive advantage. Nayyar (1997: 28) summarizes the logic of the world trade rules as follows:

national borders should not matter for trade flows and capital flows but should be clearly demarcated for technology flows and labor flows. It follows that the developing countries would provide access to their markets without corresponding access to technology and would accept capital mobility without a corresponding provision of labor mobility.

This anti-poor bias of the rules of the game, resulting in deepening inequality across the world, stems from the current situation in the global political economy, whereby 'global bodies tend to be either irrelevant if representative, or if relevant, to be dominated by the rich' (Milanovic, 2005: 150). In drawing your attention to the relationship between the key institutions in contemporary IB and the trends in world poverty and inequality, we would like to encourage you to reflect upon whether and how the international institutions discussed above could act in the interest of all parties affecting and affected by IB, rather than mainly in that of rich nations and MNEs.

alternative institutions of and against IB

In addition to the major government-sponsored institutions with a direct link to IB activities, there are a vast array of other bodies and coalitions that are involved to a greater or lesser extent, and with varying degrees of impact. The most widely recognized international institution is probably the United Nations (UN). Whilst the main body of the UN acts primarily at a macro-political level, it is the umbrella organization for a number of agencies that are concerned with IB. The International Labour Organization (ILO) is charged with 'advancing opportunities for women and men to obtain decent and productive work in conditions of freedom, equity, security and human dignity' (ILO, no date).

Another UN agency that has relevance to employment conditions, in particular, for those who work in shipping and related industries, is the International Maritime Organization (IMO). Again, the stated aims indicate that the organization has an interest in supporting the development of better working conditions. So, the UN is seen to encompass two agencies that have an interest in improving conditions in the ship-breaking industry that we discuss in various parts of this book. Whilst the ILO has sponsored several critical studies of ship-breaking (e.g. Rahman and Ullah, 1999), it has not thus far brought about any fundamental change to it. Funding for the IMO's work is provided by ship registration nations in proportion to their fleet tonnage, which has led Greenpeace (2003) to posit that it is 'largely beholden to the shipping and oil industries'. In recognizing that it has produced little or no change to conditions in the industry, the IMO itself acknowledges that it 'has plenty of teeth but some of them don't bite' (IMO, 2002).

There are a number of social movements that confront the prevalent model of globalization. Amongst them, the most vocal include the anti-globalization movement, feminist movements, organized labour and environmental movements (Roberts and Hite, 2000). In addition, a range of non-governmental organizations (NGOs) engage in analysis of and challenge the 'normal' practices of MNEs, highlighting examples of labour exploitation (see War on Want, 2006), resource depletion (e.g. Greenpeace) and environmental degradation (e.g. Friends of the Earth). There are also a variety of organizations that take direct action against certain IB activities. For example, the Sea Shepherd organization takes disruptive measures against Japanese whaling and other activities that are deadly to marine life. Resistance to the activities of MNEs also arises on the part of local communities, in response to specific issues. In 1999–2000, the people of Cochabamba in Bolivia formed a resistance movement which succeeded in overturning the government's decision to privatize the water supply. This grassroots action demonstrated that it is possible to prevent the takeover of public services by powerful private sector agents, in this case a consortium that comprised a US multinational and Bolivian companies with links to the political elite of the country (Otto and Böhm, 2006).

Starting with mass demonstrations at the WTO meeting in Seattle in December 1999 (BBC, 1999), the last decade has seen a rise in protests against the increasing spread and power of the institutions of neo-liberal market economics. Whilst not constituting a single unified body that is 'for' something, participating groups and individuals challenge the prevailing model of globalization, Americanization, 'McDonaldization' (Ritzer, 1995) and the hegemony of MNEs. Whilst arguably fragmented and acting in isolation of each other, these groups have come together and shown their power outside meetings of the G8 and WTO, for example, in Seattle in 1999, Geneva in 2003 and Gleneagles in 2005.

Since 2001, the World Social Forum has constituted a platform for the exchange of ideas and engagement in projects directed at the forces of capitalism and imperialism. The emergence of such a forum for debate and discussion at a global level can be considered as an example of the possibility of a new global order that offers an alternative to the current paradigm. In addition to evidence from the activities of social movements, such a possibility has been theorized by contemporary intellectuals, for example, Hardt and Negri (2004), who see the potential for counter-capitalism through the establishment of a language and a communication network that asserts the desire of the 'multitude' for a new socio-economic order.

conclusion

In this chapter, we have offered an overview of the institutional frameworks of contemporary IB, exposing the role of the Bretton Woods conference in establishing the current transnational economic institutions. We started by explaining the origins and development of the international monetary system, and pointed to its roots in British imperialism. We discussed the main principles of the Bretton Woods system of exchange rates, and outlined the reasons behind its failure. Moreover, we provided some recent examples of the mechanisms by which currency exchange rates are determined.

Following our discussion of the international monetary system, we introduced the major transnational institutions underpinning global economic activity, namely, the IMF, the World Bank and the WTO. In addition to providing background information about their aims and activities, we presented some of the criticisms which, over time, have been directed at them. In particular, we highlighted how the principles of the IMF, the World Bank and the WTO are grounded in the doctrine of neo-liberalism and we have commented on how, outside the discourse of neo-liberal thinking, these have been criticized and challenged. Most notably, we have introduced discussion about the impact of these three institutions upon the economic situation of developing countries.

We have also considered different forms and institutions of economic integration. Here, we have explained the principles behind, and have given examples of, the main forms of such integration, including the free trade area, customs union, common market, economic union and political union. Moreover, we have articulated some of the critical arguments put forward in relation to economic integration. In particular, we have considered how regional economic blocs contribute to maintaining and reinforcing unequal power relations between nation states within the contemporary international political economy.

Finally, we have given a necessarily brief overview of some of the wide range of social movements and organizations that challenge the current model of globalization and the activities of companies engaged in IB. In doing so, we trust that we have raised your awareness of the fact that the current institutional frameworks of IB are contested, and should not be assumed to constitute the underpinnings of the only possible present and future social and economic order. For those who wish to read more on these alternatives, we would point to web resources such as www.brettonwoodsproject.org, www.globalissues.org, www.motherjones.com and www.southcentre.org as well as those NGOs that we have mentioned above.

5

The International Business Organization

introduction

So far, in this book, we have discussed the origins of international business, theories of IB and the supranational agencies that define the context and rules of IB. This discussion has, necessarily, been to a large extent rooted in economics, since IB has been primarily viewed as an economic activity. Notwithstanding its early grounding in trade between countries, contemporary understanding of IB for many will be linked to thinking on the multinational enterprise (MNE), on global brands such as McDonald's, Nokia and Bosch, or to corporate scandals such as those involving Enron and Worldcom. In this chapter, we discuss the origins and development of MNEs and, in particular, how they have been and remain more than just organizations of commerce, which can be seen as benign in the fields of business, politics, society and environment, and frequently have close links to the political agendas of their home countries. We look at both historical and more recent examples of the international firm in order to explain its significance.

colonial expansion and the internationalization of business

Whilst international trade has existed for millennia across the globe, the emergence of the international firm can be traced to

European colonial expansion in the era of geographical exploration. The historical importance of the connection between political interests of the nation state and internationalization of commercial organizations can be illustrated through the examples of the Honourable East India Company (HEIC) and the Dutch East India Company (Vereenigde Oostindische Compagnie, or VOC). These privately owned commercial organizations were key drivers of and actors in English and Dutch colonial expansion, respectively, and in the spread of capitalism. The HEIC, with 125 merchant shareholders, was granted a Royal Charter on 31 December 1600, and for over 250 years in various forms it grew and developed to the stage where its officials practically ruled the sub-continent on behalf of the British government. The company initially established trading rights with Emperor Jahangir, ruler of the Mughal Empire, and this gave the HEIC exclusive rights to develop bases and to acquire local goods and resources, such as tea, silk and dyes, in return for providing European luxury goods to the emperors and their courts.

Over its history, the company maintained a relationship with Parliament that saw its powers ebb and flow, but at various times it held rights to mint currency, acquire territories, establish its own military forces, exercise legal powers, and make war and peace on behalf of the country. By the mid-eighteenth century, the Mughal Empire had disintegrated, to be replaced by various regional states. Whilst this was not a period of instability, members of the HEIC were able to exploit the fragmentation and assert their power and influence. Competing British and French colonialists initially allied themselves with different local factions in order to seek to maximize their territorial advantage. The British forces, led by Robert Clive, succeeded in taking control of Bengal. As the British asserted their power, company governors became state governors, with company governor-general Richard, later Marquess, Wellesley using military power in order to impose hegemonic British rule over an area that latterly extended from modern-day Burma/Myanmar in the south-east to Afghanistan in the north-west. During the 100 years of its existence, the company became more an agent of government than a trading company, and after the loss of its trade monopoly in 1813 it ceased all trading activities. After running up mounting losses on its administrative and military functions, it was finally nationalized and dissolved in 1874. However, its administrative legacy laid the basis for the development of the British Civil Service.

During the period in which the HEIC established English, then British, colonialism in India, the VOC similarly played a leading role in Dutch colonization of South East Asia. Whilst the HEIC was a wholly British venture, the VOC was the world's first multinational enterprise, with shareholders from Germany and what are now Belgium and Luxembourg. By the end of the seventeenth century, with establishments in areas that include modern Bangladesh, Iran, Malaysia, Taiwan, Thailand and southern China, the company not only had a substantial establishment of merchant ships and employees, but also a fleet of 40 warships and an army of 10,000 soldiers. In 1641, following the expulsion of Portuguese traders by the Japanese, the VOC established a trading post on the artificial island of Dejima in Nagasaki Bay. This was, from 1641 until 1853, the only means by which Europeans could trade with Japan. In addition to its peaceful trading activities, however, the company was implicated in the use of forced repatriation and the killing of native populations as a tool of business development in the Banda Islands, part of modern Indonesia.

These two examples illustrate how geographical expansion of nation states in pursuit of their colonialist and imperialist ambitions was interlinked with the growth of companies and the spread of capitalist enterprise across the world. The establishment of the conditions for these companies to trade in and from the new territories was made possible through the use of military power, sometimes without the explicit sanction of the home country government. In the rest of this chapter we will look not only at the growth and expansion of the contemporary MNE and its social, economic and environmental impacts, but also at the present-day linkage of some MNEs to the government of their country of origin, and to the application of military force in their countries of operation.

technological development and the internationalization of business

Looking at the growth of IB from an historical perspective, as well as in the political context, the development of technology has been of primary importance in creating conditions for nation states to colonize overseas territories, and for capitalist organizations to extend their operations internationally. Steger (2003) explains how the expansionist aspirations of European powers were assisted by the invention of mechanized printing, developments in wind and water mill technologies, advancements in navigation techniques and sea transportation, and the development of extensive postal systems.

Over time, the ability to transport goods and people facilitated the internationalization of business, as railways, mechanized shipping and, more recently, intercontinental air transport were developed. Furthermore, the invention of the telegraph and, later, the telephone and radio provided vastly increased speed of communication across the world, enabling both governments and businesses to control their activities from a central point more effectively. By 1866 Europe and North America were connected by undersea telegraph cable, whilst by 1890 all the major colonies of the British Empire were cabled from the UK. Subsequently, undersea telegraph cables were replaced by telephone cables and, in parallel, radio communication was developed. Now, of course, we have the Internet and satellite-based global communications networks.

Advances in a range of technologies have seen the development of new ways of doing business, new businesses in existing fields, and wholly new types of business. Examples of these three developments include, respectively, Internet banking, low-cost airlines, and Google and eBay. In recent decades, major development has taken place in the fields of information technology (IT) and telecommunications – often referred to jointly as information and communications technologies (ICTs). New ICTs, however, are not the only, or the major, technological enablers of internationalization. Before we address their contribution, we will point to a recent development of earlier technologies that has had a major impact on the growth of IB.

In the field of shipping, the period since the Second World War has seen the development of new forms of mass sea transportation that have enabled organizations to engage in global transfer of a wide range of raw materials and finished products. The development of containerization has allowed the growth of international logistics networks for moving large amounts of goods at relatively low cost in small units. Modularized containers are carried not just on ships, through a global network of major ports like Singapore, Rotterdam and New Orleans, but also by rail and road – in a single unit from their source to their final destination. In addition, the major petroleum refining companies now distribute oil products globally in 'very large crude carriers' (VLCCs), whilst automobile companies move cars, trucks and other vehicles around the world on huge 'roll-on, roll-off' (Ro-Ro) vessels.

There have been major developments in air transportation during the same period but, whilst it offers speed of global goods movement, it remains much more expensive than sea transportation, and therefore is used by companies primarily for the purpose of moving people or those products which need to be transported rapidly and in relatively small and high value packages. Whilst developments in logistics and transportation technology have facilitated the growth of international business and, as such, benefited companies, they have not had an equally positive effect on stakeholders within IB, in particular through their detrimental impact upon the natural environment. In recent times, air transportation has been subject to criticism for its rising level of carbon emissions, in large part due to the growth in low-cost airlines across the world. However, a recent report from the Institute for Physics and Atmosphere in Wessling, Germany (Vidal, 2007) outlines how carbon dioxide emissions from shipping, which carries 90% of world trade, are double those of aviation and could rise by as much as 75% over the next fifteen years as world trade continues to expand. The issue of global warming and climate change is no longer contested, and there is a clear link between these and the level of emissions. In this context, serious questions need to be asked as to whether we should celebrate the opportunities for global market expansion and production dispersal by international business or, rather, be concerned about the impact of the generated environmental damage upon the future of planet Earth. In our view, the environmental effects resulting from the internationalization of businesses, especially those operating at a global level, create an urgent need for thinking about what kind of, and to what extent, IB practices should be encouraged and considered as positive developments.

The contribution of new ICTs in the last few decades has grown exponentially, as the power and speed of technologies has multiplied. The introduction of mobile phones, laptop computers and integrated mobile ICTs, along with Internet development, enables individuals and businesses to communicate almost instantaneously from any location and to pass vast amounts of data and information securely. However, the internationalization of business activity and, in particular, the growth of MNEs would not have been possible without advances in technology that have taken place over centuries. At the outset, transport and logistics developments made it possible for capitalist organizations to reach overseas markets, whilst improvements in production technologies also enabled them to increase output in order to serve these new markets. Developments in communications, which initially supported exchange of information and the execution of control by organizations, have extended with recent ICT innovations, to facilitate the instantaneous transfer of both information and capital at a global level. The latter has, in turn, contributed to the financialization of the contemporary economy. It should be noted, however, that new ICTs have not only supported new ways for businesses and their people to organize globally, but they have also provided the means for emerging counter forces to organize and rally support against governments and businesses, and their activities. The types of counter-organization that we outlined in Chapter 4 rely to a great extent upon open systems of global communication and networking in order to further their causes and to summon support.

New ICTs have also enabled an increase in international financial flows. Coupled with financial liberalization, these technologies have made it possible for companies and individuals in one country to purchase shares, finance property development or borrow and locate funds in banks abroad to a much greater extent than in the past. Whilst the growth of international finance constitutes a significant aspect of the development of IB activities in recent times, it has also brought about a stronger drive for shareholder value and a higher frequency of financial crises, affecting economies of both rich and developing countries. As Glyn (2006) points out, this has resulted in the emergence of new groups of 'winners' – mainly chief executives and successful speculators on financial markets – as well as 'losers' – those workers whose jobs, working conditions and pensions have been put at greater risk than before.

Having considered the historical antecedents of the contemporary MNE along with the political, economic and technological factors that have enabled and supported its growth, we now consider the ways in which firms go about internationalizing.

internationalization of companies

As Porter (1985) points out, firms may adopt a number of strategies in seeking to gain 'competitive advantage' through internationalizing. A central theme of contemporary internationalization is the drive to configure the company 'value chain' (Porter, 1985) in order to increase efficiency, make most effective use of resources and, hence, maximize profits. Traditionally, internationalization of the firm has been seen to proceed according to the model of gradual involvement in international activities. This model suggests that companies wishing to internationalize normally start from employing market entry strategies that require a low level of engagement in operations abroad, before moving on to more advanced forms of IB presence. It is usually assumed that firms will decide to grow internationally for a number of reasons, which might include an anticipated increase in profitability, or an expectation of delivering a product or service that is not currently available in a foreign market. Alternatively, they may desire to take advantage of expertise they might have about a foreign market, to benefit from tax subsidies available abroad or to generate economies of scale through increasing production to meet international demand. Moreover, companies may choose to start operating abroad in order to respond to competitive pressures, to counter the decline in demand within the domestic market, to utilize excess production capacity, or to seize the opportunity to expand abroad through serving a foreign market located within a close geographic or psychological distance from the domestic one, and which, thereby, can be entered relatively easily. In order to internationalize, firms may choose between a range of 'modes of market entry', such as exporting and importing, licensing, franchising, short- and long-term alliances, subcontracting, and merger and acquisition. In the space of this book, we cannot discuss all of these in depth, and would refer the interested reader to texts on international business (e.g. Czinkota et al., 2005; Daniels et al., 2007; Rugman and Collinson, 2006).

As with many other theories and concepts in the field of IB, within these market entry modes the firm is the central actor whose potential advantages and risks are considered. However, it needs to be remembered that the selected strategies of internationalization are not without influence upon the rest of the stakeholders in IB. In addition to the previously discussed environmental impacts of global logistics and transportation that will occur, to a differing extent, in the case of each of the market entry modes, effects upon society should not be ignored. In configuring their value chains internationally and globally through sub-contracting, firms are able to take advantage of geographical locations of production with the lowest cost structures. Those who work for sub-contractor companies of MNEs (e.g. the producers of the majority of consumer goods) are often based in developing countries and are employed at a low wage and under precarious working conditions. Since they are not the direct employees of the MNE but of the sub-contractor, the multinational company which benefits from their labour does not have the legal responsibility for ensuring that the labour practices of the sub-contractor are the same as those that the MNE would have to obey in its home country.

Another example of a possible negative impact of a market entry strategy upon a party other than the shareholders of the companies involved can be found in the case of merger and acquisition. This strategy of internationalization can benefit firms not only through providing them with access to new markets, resources and expertise, but can potentially lead to lowering costs through reducing the number of employees. Where this happens, the post-merger or post-acquisition company may have lower staff costs than the two entities prior to the merger or acquisition. This, at the same time, will mean the loss of jobs for a number of people, loss of the source of income for them and their families, and may require government to provide the individuals affected with unemployment benefits, if such a safety net is offered in the particular country. Moreover, merger and acquisition activity at an international level can contribute to an increase in the market power of companies pursuing this strategy. Some consequences of this, for example a higher influence of the firm upon the price levels in its industry, may disadvantage the customers, who will have to pay a higher price for the products than they would have to if prices were determined under more competitive conditions.

From the outline of the various strategies of internationalization, it would be possible to infer that through a process of gradual expansion, MNEs grow into evenly geographically spread entities, with a similar type of presence across the world. One needs to remember, however, that despite the globalization of economic activity by companies, control over the world's MNEs is executed from relatively few locations. The top 20 companies in the *Fortune 500* global list of top companies by revenue generation for 2006 includes ten firms with headquarters in Europe, eight based in the USA, plus one each from China and Japan (Fortune, 2007). These examples lead us to a consideration of the economic and political power of MNEs in the contemporary world.

economic and political power of multinational enterprises

When asked to give the names of well-known MNEs, most people will immediately think in terms of global consumer brands, such as Coca-Cola, McDonald's, or Nike. However, few are aware of the scale of contemporary MNEs' economic power, and of the fact that their revenues frequently exceed the GDP of entire countries. For example, Wal-Mart and Exxon Mobil, with revenues of $351 billion and $347 billion, respectively in 2006, would lie at numbers 22 and 23 in the list of countries, between Indonesia and Poland (World Bank, 2007), whilst the revenues of Royal Dutch Shell, BP and General Motors equate to the GDPs of countries like Austria, Denmark and Thailand, respectively. In addition, few realize that the list of the largest commercial players in contemporary IB (other than Wal-Mart) is dominated by petroleum refiners. Of the *Fortune 500* top 10 global businesses by revenue in 2006, six operated in this field: Exxon Mobil, Royal Dutch Shell, BP, Chevron, ConocoPhillips and Total. In addition to generating the largest revenues, companies within petroleum refining were the world's most profitable, with Exxon Mobil and Royal Dutch Shell topping the list.

Whilst the list of top companies is currently dominated by firms from the 'developed' economies, there is evidence of the growth of MNEs from the 'emerging' economies, particularly China. Two of the world's top 25 revenue earners (Fortune, 2007) are Sinopec and China National Petroleum, both, notably, in the petroleum refining sector. At the same time, India and

Brazil are growing powers in the global economy, which some see as pointing to a future shift in the balance of global economic power. However, we would posit that with the emergence of a global elite of mobile hyper-rich, this is not indicative of any fundamental challenge to the 'rules of the game' as they are currently configured.

The scale and spread of their resources gives these organizations vast amounts of power and influence within the spheres of both economics and politics. Whilst some critics see in the growing power of MNEs a decline in the relevance of the nation state, others point to the way in which neo-liberal governments and large capitalist organizations support each other's interests. As such, businesses sponsor political parties and electoral campaigns at a national level in order to ensure that, through lobbyists, they will influence policy making to their own advantage. For example, in the context of the Enron scandal, it was remarked how George W. Bush had previously received about $623,000 from the company to support his political campaigns (Bello, 2003). In relation to international trade regulations, businesses often benefit from the support of governments that promote their agenda of international expansion. To illustrate this point, it is worth mentioning that in May 2002, Michael Duke, Executive Vice-President of Wal-Mart, wrote to the US Trade Representative to the WTO stating that 'Countries ... should be encouraged to remove any size limitations on individual stores, numeric limits on the number of stores in the country and geographic limitations on store locations in the country'. It was 'requested' that this be adopted as the official 'negotiating strategy' (Simms, 2007: 177).

The influence of MNEs over international policy making by the national governments of the countries of their headquarters is particularly evident when these governments decide to pursue the corporate agenda, even when it comes at the expense of societies in poor countries. For example, despite acknowledging that trade liberalization contributes to exacerbating poverty in developing countries, Tony Blair's government pushed for opening up the product and service markets in developing countries. In doing this, the UK government chose to represent 'the business agenda of British industrialists and City of London lobby groups, especially those keen to take over the banking and insurance sectors of new markets in the developing world' (War on Want, 2007), rather than to support policy making that would help reduce global poverty.

In addition to their involvements in political lobbying, MNEs have a record – some might say a questionable record – of funding scientific research that supports their vested interests. The tobacco industry has a history of sponsoring research that seeks to show that the generally recognized health risks of smoking are over-rated or non-existent (Carnall, 1996; Goodchild and Hodgson, 2006). Similarly, ExxonMobil is reported (Adam, 2006; Greenpeace, 2007) to be a major funder of groups that are labelled 'climate change sceptics'. Overall, the effects of the activities of MNEs go far beyond their bottom line. Through their broader economic and political impacts, large capitalist organizations influence everybody in society to an extent that many may not realize. To illustrate this point, in the following section we consider a variety of social impacts of Wal-Mart, the world's largest – in terms of revenues and the number of employees – private company.

▬▬▬ rhetoric and reality of Wal-Mart

The example of Wal-Mart is worthy of consideration because of the insights it offers into the relationship between the organization of business activities by MNEs and the direction of change within contemporary society. Founded in the small American town of Bentonville, Arkansas in 1962 by Sam Walton, the retail chain Wal-Mart now has 2,285 retail outlets located in 15 countries. In these, products from 70 countries around the globe are sold by over 1.8 million 'associates' (Wal-Mart, 2006).

Wal-Mart (2006) presents itself in a positive light in relation to its economic, social and environmental credentials. The company emphasizes its positive role, working closely with its suppliers, creating opportunities for its employees worldwide, providing savings for consumers – contributing not only to its own growth, but also 'giv(ing) the world an opportunity to see what it's like to save and do better' (Wal-Mart, 2006: 13). In setting out its commitment to people, the company states how 'Wal-Mart offers tremendous opportunities for [its] associates to develop their professional skills and pursue a long-term career ... where people are treated honestly and with respect' (Wal-Mart, 2006: 1). It stresses that it has 'a responsibility and an opportunity to improve the quality of life in every community [it] serve[s]'. It also highlights its commitment to sustainability and environmental responsibility, stating that it 'can make the earth a better place for all of us and that [it] can be an efficient, profitable enterprise' (Wal-Mart, 2006: 8).

Wal-Mart's bright image of itself is not, however, shared by others. Whilst the company highlights its contribution to the communities where it sets up operations, it has been pointed out (Miller, 2004) that, with its low wage structure, many of its employees rely upon government health insurance and school meal programmes that cost the US taxpayer over $1.5 billion per annum. Goetz and Swaminathan (2006) refer to a 2001 report by *BusinessWeek*, in which it was stated that the average annual income of a Wal-Mart associate, at $13,861, was below the US poverty line for a family of three. From their own empirical study, they conclude that counties that either had or saw the establishment of Wal-Mart stores 'experienced greater increases (or smaller decreases) in family-poverty rates during the 1990s economic boom period' (Goetz and Swaminathan, 2006: 211).

Whilst Wal-Mart proclaims its environmental credentials, there are numerous accounts (see University of Wisconsin System, 2004; Wal-Mart Watch, 2005) of it being subject to punitive fines for breaking US environmental and safety laws. However, environmental degradation is not confined to the direct action of the company itself, but is also a side-effect of its global procurement strategy in pursuit of lowering the cost of goods to its customers, as it ships vast amount of produce around the world from its low-cost suppliers to its market outlets.

In pointing out that Wal-Mart does not bear 'the full economic and social cost of its business practices', Goetz and Swaminathan (2006: 223) contend that the company 'transfers income from the working poor and from taxpayers ... to stockholders and the heirs of the Wal-Mart fortune, as well as to consumers'. Of course, the transfer of income from the 'working poor and from taxpayers' to consumers is, to a large extent, illusory – the 'new' income being generated by the lower costs of produce, largely derived from the reduced cost of the associates' labour. The exacerbation of poverty and inequalities in society, along with environmental damage, are happening in the name of societal values of increased consumer choice, purchasing power and consumption – a project in which we are all implicated. As Fishman (2007: 247) points out: 'Wal-Mart is not just a reflection of ... society and values. It is a mirror of us as individuals.'

organization and militarization

The above discussion of the economic and political power of MNEs in the contemporary world allows us to realize that there are parallels between the past and the present, in relation to the interdependencies of politics and business. As mentioned earlier in this chapter, historically, the common interests of governments and private capital in pursuit of geographic expansion led to political domination of the many by the few, and to the development of capitalism as the dominant economic system. Similarly, the agenda of neo-liberalism in the present time sees the locus of control of world trade lying with a coalition of developed world governments and big business. Additionally, as we have pointed to the role of military power and action in the growth of international trade in previous centuries, we can identify links between government, business and both the arms trade and military action in the current IB arena (see Sharma and Kumar, 2003).

Over the past two decades, concerns have been raised by various groups (e.g. Corporate Watch, 2002; Ridgeway, 2003) about the ties between developed world governments and MNEs in the fields of both military action by oppressive regimes and the exploitation of the aftermath of war. In the UK context, the MNE BAE Systems has been the subject of a number of investigations in relation to the sale of military hardware, including fighter aircraft, to countries which were criticized for oppressive action against their own minority populations. BAE Systems defines itself (http://www.baesystems.com/) as 'the premier global defence and aerospace company' and has business operations in Europe, North America, the Middle East, Africa and Australasia. In the 1990s, the company, along with the Conservative government of the time, was subject to a wave of criticism for selling 16 of its Hawk 'multi-role combat aircraft' to President Suharto's regime in Indonesia when it was repressing the population of East Timor through military action, including alleged air attacks on civilian targets by Hawks supplied previously (Monbiot, 1996). Amongst the leading critics was the Labour Opposition MP Robin Cook, who, as Foreign Secretary in Tony Blair's Labour government after 1997, renewed the export licence (*Guardian Unlimited*, 1999). Similarly, in 1998, the company sold a range of weaponry to Turkey, a country which was then accused by the Council of Europe of having a history of 'repeated and serious human rights violations' (Wrigley, 2000), including military offensives against the civilian Kurdish population.

In addition to examples of MNE involvement in enabling oppressive military action, the aftermath of the US-led invasions of Afghanistan and Iraq has raised many questions about the activities of private companies in both the lucrative 'rebuilding' programmes and in the provision of 'private security' – what some say would in the past have been referred to as mercenary armies. In relation to rebuilding in Iraq, US multinational companies such as Bechtel and Parsons (both major contributors to Republican Party funds (BBC, 2004), have been awarded billions of US dollars of contracts, albeit that '[t]he Bush administration rejected suggestions that there was a connection between donations and deals'. With reference to private security, *The Washington Post*

(Fainura, 2007) reported that 'billions of dollars in U.S. military and State Department contracts' underpinned the provision of 20–30,000 armed contractors by more than 100 security companies in order to 'offset chronic troop shortages'. These contractors have been involved in gathering military intelligence (Fainaru and Klein, 2007), have been implicated in rape and torture at the notorious Abu Ghraib prison (Conachy, 2004), and have been reported as 'taking hundreds of casualties that have been underreported and sometimes concealed' (Fainaru, 2007).

Further examples of IB activities underpinned by military action have been highlighted in reports that point to links between MNEs from the USA, Europe and China, and mining and resource extraction in the world's richest country in mineral reserves, the Democratic Republic of Congo (DRC) (see Herman et al., 2002; Lobe, 2003). The DRC provides a source of ores used in tin production and industrial diamonds, and is the major source of coltan, an ore that supplies essential minerals for use in the consumer electronics that are central to developed world lives, including mobile phones and computer gaming systems. However, this is a country that is ravaged by internal strife, where the civilian population is subjected to systematic pillage, rape and torture by soldiers of the private armies of a host of warlords, some supported by the armies of neighbouring countries. This is a population for whom there is no reward from the country's vast wealth (see Amnesty International, 2003).

conclusion

In this chapter, we have looked at the major commercial actor in IB – the MNE – from an historical and a contemporary perspective. We have, in particular, focused on the link between firms operating internationally and the spheres of politics, the economy, society and the environment. By reference to historical examples of the HEIC and VOC, we have explained how, over time, the growth of international companies has been facilitated by and contributed to the geographical expansion of the European powers and to the development of capitalism as the dominant economic system.

We have pointed to key developments in technology that have influenced the growth of IB. We have also drawn attention to advances in transportation and logistics, production technologies and communication, and to their role in promoting IB activities through enabling time and cost-efficient transfer of goods, people, information and capital. Following our discussion of the historical influences on the growth of MNEs, we have addressed issues relating to the functioning of capitalist organizations in contemporary IB. Having listed the various modes of market entry available to firms, we have commented on how some of them impact stakeholders other than the companies' shareholders. We have also reflected upon the economic and political power of MNEs. Moreover, we have elaborated on the case of Wal-Mart, as an exemplification of the problematic nature of corporate success, whereby international growth and high financial performance, coupled with low prices for the consumer, have come at a high cost for the workers, the taxpayers and the environment.

Furthermore, we have drawn attention to an additional aspect of IB that is absent from most of the mainstream accounts – how MNEs and consumers from developed economies benefit from military conflict. Highlighting the past and present interdependencies between companies operating internationally and politics, the economy, society and the environment has allowed us to show that, through their diverse impacts, IB activities are not just relevant to the firms involved in them and their shareholders, but to everybody in society, both in the present and in the future.

Part III

Managing in the International Business Environment

6

Delivering Goods and Services

Bottled water is so much environmental madness. ... It's absolutely absurd to be putting this very heavy bulky and yet supercheap product in bottles which weigh almost as much as the product and carting these around the world.

Matt Phillips, Friends of the Earth

introduction

To this point, we have developed a discussion of IB by considering its historical development and its status in the present time from the perspectives of a range of parties. We have not, thus far, taken cognizance of what it means to be a manager involved in IB activity. Part of the IB canon, as presented in the majority of textbooks, includes discussion of the functional aspects of management in the international context. Our aim in this section is to address those elements of IB which fall within the subject area referred to as 'international management'. Specifically, in the limited space available, we will provide a broad overview of issues relating to the design and delivery of goods and services internationally: research and development (R&D), marketing, logistics and supply chain management. In addition, we will discuss aspects of the finance, accounting and governance activities associated with IB transactions. Finally, we will outline key issues relating to managing people in the international firm. Our engagement with these aspects of international management will, again, aim to offer a range of perspectives on the implications and impacts of international management practice, challenging some of the unstated assumptions that underpin the mangerialist rhetoric.

global research and development

In the context of contemporary IB, R&D activities are seen to contribute to organizations' competitiveness in both operational and strategic terms. At an operational level, R&D investment is considered to support the identification of new product opportunities, of new ways of applying existing products, and of technological advances in production processes. The outcomes of any or all of these are potentially conducive to the promotion of increased productivity and hence profitability. At the strategic level, investment in R&D is seen as an essential approach to building and maintaining competitive advantage over other organizations in the same market. This is the case, in particular, in technology-intensive industries, such as pharmaceuticals, aircraft manufacture and telecommunications. In order to deliver products that will be selected by the consumer over those of competitors, companies aim constantly to build and maintain a lead in new product development. In the music industry, the last thirty or so years has seen a journey from vinyl through cartridges, cassettes and CDs to MP3 downloads from the Internet. Similarly, a half-century has seen a move from the then Chairman of IBM forecasting a total world demand for about six computers to the present day, where one household may have this number! Whilst it is a crucial element of organizational success, R&D also represents a high cost to businesses. As such, large multinational organizations are better able to support major R&D projects than are smaller enterprises, making R&D an issue of concern to those studying international business. Research and development is, in itself, a major international business activity that affects and is affected by a range of social, economic and environmental factors, but its essence is in providing future products and services that respond to targeted market needs.

As can readily be recognizsed, R&D requires specialist knowledge and a high level of skills in addition to the financial investment. As such, the majority of R&D effort is concentrated in countries that are able to offer the necessary knowledge and skills bases in their workforce. In contemporary business, this may lead to the development of technology clusters, where firms engaging in the same field of business locate close to each other in order to take advantage of these resources. Examples of such clustering include the US Silicon Valley, Scotland's Silicon Glen and Malaysia's Multimedia Super Corridor (MSC). As the final example illustrates, R&D is not the exclusive domain of the traditional 'developed' economies. In fact, as China, at present, graduates more engineers and scientists than any other country, many companies locate their R&D activities there.

As we have pointed out, R&D is an expensive undertaking and, as such, organizations do not lightly engage in activities that are high-risk and unlikely to provide a financial return on investment. The logic of directing R&D spending towards low-risk and high-return developments is understandable from the point of view of profit-maximization by commercial organizations. However, it has its pitfalls when considered from the perspective of a variety of stakeholders. For example, in the field of pharmaceuticals, it is known that new drug development takes a considerable amount of time and is a high-risk and high-cost undertaking. For these reasons, firms within the pharmaceutical industry tend to concentrate their resources on research and development of those medicines that are guaranteed to bring a return on the R&D investment. At the same time, investment in those medicines that are seen to be unattractive in terms of profitability is unlikely to occur. Both the World Health Organization (WHO) and the academic community have expressed concern that market-driven R&D of new pharmaceuticals leaves a lot of the health problems in the world unaddressed. One study (Trouiller et al., 2002) highlighted that of 1,393 pharmaceuticals brought to market between 1975 and 1999, only 16 provided treatments for tropical diseases and tuberculosis.

Whilst tuberculosis may be neglected by the major investors in medical research, being seen as a 'low-return' disease, in 2005 alone the WHO estimated that TB caused 1.6 million deaths worldwide and pointed out that the incidence of this disease is on the increase across less developed economic regions. As infectious diseases that result in high mortality rates in these areas remain by and large ignored, the major drug investment is targeted at western health problems, from cancer to depression and to male sex organ malfunction, at those areas where products respond to the needs of the paying and profit-generating population of the west.

international marketing

Marketing is defined by Harvard Business School (2008) as the means by which firms 'attract customers by learning about potential needs, helping to develop products that customers want, creating awareness, and communicating benefits' and, thereafter, they 'retain [customers] by ensuring that they get good value, appropriate service, and a stream of future products'. Within this framework, the role of marketing research and marketing management is, respectively, to enable the identification and the fulfilment of these needs and wants by the organization. In theory, this model presents a business/customer relationship based upon mutual interest and equal power. However, we would challenge this notion.

International marketing research is generally aimed at finding out about opportunities for selling a company's products and services to customers based in different countries. This involves identifying similarities, as well as differences, between the various target markets and the home market. The aim is, as far as possible, to enable application of a relatively standardized 'marketing mix' (product, price, promotion and distribution) in all country markets, exploiting economies of scale. In the field of marketing research, differences between markets – which will result in variations in consumers' needs and wants – can be identified along three dimensions, namely physical distance, psychic distance and economic distance. The first of these relates to geographic distance between home and target markets. The second encompasses variations in language, culture, tradition and societal norms. Economic distance incorporates consideration of the financial costs, benefits and risks involved in exchange between markets and, ultimately, the customer's ability to pay. These three types of distance are addressed by companies through the application of marketing management strategies, which in the international context will encompass decisions regarding the extent to which the elements of marketing mix will be standardized across markets or adapted to suit local conditions. We are not going to elaborate here on the specifics of applying various international marketing strategies. Rather, we wish to point to a few problems we see occurring where the concepts and practices of international marketing are confronted with broader societal issues.

The key problematic element of marketing strategy for us is that it conceptualizes people merely as 'consumers' rather than as partners, parents, children, or citizens. As such, differences between groups and individuals, along with characteristics of age, gender, race and income, become mere 'issues' to be addressed in the marketing design – either as problems to be overcome or as opportunities to be exploited. Within this regime, those who have insufficient disposable income to purchase the firm's offerings fall off the radar screen. At the same time, any issues of social conflict and injustice that are considered are viewed in relation to their implications for the company's ability to market its products. An example of the dehumanizing and disembodying of consumers is seen in Charles Hill's (2007) use of Jordan's (2000) article on the problems of marketing to black Brazil. Hill uses the paper to show the importance of recognizing that contemporary Brazilian society is multiracial and that this presents companies, for example, in the cosmetics industry, with the opportunity to target new market segments. Marketers are presented with the challenge of how to develop subtle techniques for targeting consumers with different skin tones. The plethora of skin tones in Brazil is shown to be historically grounded, but the history of racial relations is presented as benign since, rather than 'exclud[ing] blacks from voting or ... segregating the races ... the government encouraged inter-marriage between whites and blacks in order to "bleach" society' (Hill, 2007: 587).

The approach that we see here in international marketing is one that presents racial difference as an opportunity, but places it within the context of a project of long-term de-differentiation of the population. As such, the globalization agenda of convergence and monoculturalism is evident. Whilst we can identify trends towards social, cultural and economic convergence globally, we must point out that, overall, economic differences between and within countries are deepening year on year. This also suggests opportunities for expansion to the international marketer through identifying global market segmentation. Looking at luxury goods like Prada fashions and Rolex watches, market growth may be achieved at a global level whilst maintaining the mystique of exclusiveness. This also allows the new global elite to build identity and commonality, whilst reinforcing its socio-economic detachment from other groups in society. Within this culture of 'conspicuous consumption', the task of international marketing researchers becomes that of identifying potential market segments whilst ensuring that the company's product retains its exclusiveness.

Whilst, to this point, we have addressed the mainstream of marketing in the IB context, we would now point to Glenn Morgan's (2003) challenge to the definition of marketing as underpinned by the concept of satisfying consumers' needs and wants. This challenges the implicit assumption that, through addressing these needs and wants, marketing is doing 'good' for people and that it has, therefore, some ethical basis. There are a few problems with this basic assumption. For example, in relation to the activity of MNEs, the notion of fundamental need is not subject to general agreement. Critical responses to marketing activity, particularly by some of these MNEs, point to the idea that, first, customer needs are not only identified by organizations but, also, are created by them. In the fashion industry, for example, consumers are urged to purchase clothes, shoes and accessories from the latest collections, regardless of the fact that they may already have a full wardrobe. In this context, marketing activities aim at convincing potential customers that they have a particular need which a new product or service will fulfil.

Second, it is highlighted that the products and services which are marketed at particular groups do not necessarily contribute to their welfare. In recent years, with increasing awareness of health issues and with threats of litigation, some products, such as tobacco, have become subject to restrictions and bans on marketing in developed countries whilst, at the same time, they have been at the centre of major marketing pushes in countries in Africa and other less developed countries. In another example, various reports (e.g. WHO, 2006) have highlighted how multi-national companies have actively marketed formula baby milks in various LDCs, in contravention of the World Health Assembly's 1982 Code of Conduct. This code was aimed at clarifying not only the health benefits of breast milk, but also the dangers of preparing formula milks in places where the quality of water did not fulfil necessary hygiene criteria. Despite the obvious health risk to babies, formula milks were strongly marketed and in some cases companies were shown to be providing financial and material incentives to support sales by those who were charged in their official roles with promoting the benefits of breast-feeding to mothers.

In recent years, the notion of addressing wider social issues has been incorporated into the rhetoric of mainstream marketing with the introduction of the term 'societal marketing' (see Kotler and Levy, 1969; Lazer, 1969). This term is set in a triadic relationship in which organizational, consumer and broader societal interests are balanced. However, we would challenge the notion that this ideal is realized in a business context where profit-maximization is the ultimate goal of marketing activity. Rather than being concerned with what benefits society in broad and sustainable terms, we see international marketing as constituting a central tenet of the drive to increase consumption through demand generation and reinforcement of the values of purchasing and possession.

▓▓▓▓ logistics and supply chain management

It is tempting to see the major driver of IB growth from logistics as being grounded in recent technological developments in the field of information and communications technologies (ICT). However, we would point out that advances in transportation in the last half-century, such as containerization, bulk sea transportation and the growth of mass air transportation, have been of greater significance in enabling the transfer of raw materials and finished products at a global level. International logistics is concerned with the design and management of the organizational systems involved in the flow of materials, services and information, both within the firm and in relation to its external networks across the world. In the past, when all production processes were concentrated in one location, logistics activities referred to the movement of goods and information between the producer and the consumer. In the contemporary world, business has become more diversified, with geographically dispersed networks of suppliers of materials, components and knowledge providing input to their products and services. Even a relatively simple product like a beef burger is now likely to contain ingredients sourced from across the world, transported using the logistics network of the company which markets it, and put together for customers who are likely to remain unaware of the extent to which the product they are consuming is global. As an example, Czinkota et al. (2005: 11) show how the Big Mac in Ukraine is assembled using internationally sourced ingredients that include Mexican sesame seeds, German pickles and sauce, a Russian bun, Hungarian beef, American onions and Polish cheese, with only the lettuce coming from Ukraine.

As with research and development activities, supply chain management (SCM) constitutes both an operational and a strategic element of organizational activity in the IB arena. At an operational level, organizations aim to configure the supply chain in such a way that it enables them to reduce the costs of production and to improve efficiency. Because of the availability of relatively cheap global transportation, goods produced away from the target markets can be delivered with comparative ease. Strategically, effective supply chain management is seen as an important source of competitive advantage for a company involved in IB activity, achieved through a unique configuration of international networks connecting the firm with its vendors, suppliers, customers and other involved parties. For contemporary organizations, outsourcing some of the value-adding activities to other parties within the supply chain is also seen as allowing greater flexibility and the ability to concentrate key resources on what the firm considers as its core competence. Flexibility for MNEs means not only that they are able to switch suppliers and obtain the most advantageous cost structures for materials and components, but also that they are able to divest themselves of the need to maintain inventories and stocks, since they can delegate such responsibility to the suppliers. Likewise, many IB firms are no longer responsible for maintaining the employment relationship with large parts of the productive workforce, who are working for their contracted suppliers.

Looking from a narrowly defined profit-maximization perspective, the existence of global logistics and supply chain solutions offers a lot of benefits to companies capable of configuring and coordinating their value-adding activities on a global scale. However, consideration of broader economic, social and environmental issues related to global supply chains reveals a number of problematic aspects of contemporary SCM. First, relationships within supply chains are not necessarily formed by equally independent economic agents. There is evidence that MNEs, through the bargaining power which they hold in relation to their suppliers, are in the position to dictate the terms of 'cooperation' with their business partners. As we have previously discussed (see Chapter 2), low-cost fashion retailers from the UK are able to determine the prices at which they will purchase clothing from their contractors, based upon the retailers' intended selling price rather than upon the contractors' cost levels. The pressure put upon the producers translates into low wages, long working hours and poor working and living conditions for their workforce. As a result, what is considered a source of competitive advantage for the retailer becomes a source of socio-economic disadvantage for the workers in third world countries. Moreover, MNEs' freedom to choose the most economically efficient way of configuring the supply chain at a global level enables them to transfer value-adding activities rapidly from one country to another without the need for taking into account the economic and social consequences such strategic moves have on the affected countries.

As far as the environmental consequences of global logistics and supply chain networks are concerned, the example of waste transportation from the UK to China provides an illustration of the problematic impacts. When the *MS Emma Maersk*, the world's largest container ship, first docked in the UK in December 2006, the media reported its arrival in terms both of its sheer size and also of the consumer goods it was delivering in time for Christmas. However, beyond *The Independent* newspaper (Milmo, 2007), there was little interest in the shipment that it loaded in the UK for its return journey to China. The ship took on board a cargo of Britain's fastest-growing export to China – waste. The low cost of sea transportation makes it economically feasible to ship waste materials between continents. According to the report, at £500 it costs less to send a 26-tonne container from the UK to China than by road from London to Manchester. In addition, the contents fetch a higher price in the Chinese market than domestically. According to the basic cost-based line of argumentation, the proponents of this form of IB present it as advantageous for all business parties involved. However, whilst precise figures are not available, there is clear evidence that the reprocessing, burning and burying of this waste in landfill exacts a high toll on the health of both the people who are involved in sorting it and of the wider population as well as on the condition of the environment in which it takes place. It is unrealistic to expect those directly affected to take remedial action since, for many, the alternative to the abysmal working conditions and levels of pay offered in waste processing in the coastal industrial zones of China is abject poverty in more remote parts of the country.

As can be seen from the above examples, logistics and supply chain management are important elements and enablers of IB. However, we view it as essential to consider the more problematic economic, social and environmental aspects beyond the immediate context of the firm as well as the contribution to business growth and development.

international service delivery

In the previous section, we have discussed the supply chain in relation to tangible products. However, services now constitute a major proportion of total world trade. Similar considerations apply to firms' decisions on the location and configuration of service networks as to the production of tangible goods. Additionally, many service offerings are linked to the delivery of goods, such as where the purchase of computer hardware is tied to the provision of software service support. However, whilst the elements of the production and consumption of goods are normally separated both in time and space, service delivery and the consumer experience of it are generally simultaneous, in that these two elements are inseparable. In the context of contemporary IB, this is of particular importance in the case of those services that require direct interaction of service staff and the customer, but where geographic proximity is not essential. In such cases, the parties involved might well be located in different countries on different continents, with very different cultures.

As we have pointed out above, in relation to the IT industry, software companies may choose to locate their design offices in countries other than their home market. Also, they may increasingly place their customer service sections in remote locations. Similarly, in recent years UK banks and insurance companies have moved elements of their customer service operations from Britain to countries like India, where they have access to a workforce with English language and IT skills at a lower cost than in the UK. The insurance group Norwich Union's offshoring of part of its service operations to India provides an example of this trend. In September 2006, the company announced its plan to transfer 1,000 jobs to India. The rationale behind this decision was to take advantage of the technological advances which make it possible for service organizations to rely to a lesser extent on the human element in the delivery of services to the customer. It was estimated that as a result of the offshoring exercise, the firm could potentially reduce its costs by 40% (BBC, 2006). Moreover, it was argued that the move would strengthen Norwich Union's position within the insurance industry, protecting it from potential takeover and allowing it to play an important role in consolidating the insurance market.

However, this transfer has not come without difficulties. There has been a consumer backlash against the Indian workforce's perceived lack of detailed knowledge and its inability to deal with specific requests for information. By March 2007, substantial shortcomings were revealed in the company's Indian call centres, including failure to comply with the UK Financial Service Authority's (FSA's) rules, which exposed customers to the possibility of fraud. Norwich Union's own investigations uncovered that those in charge of the Indian operations did not have a clear understanding of FSA requirements, and were using outdated customer advice training material (Foxwell, 2007b). This example of international service delivery failings illustrates how internationalization of service delivery may not necessarily be beneficial for either the organization's reputation or its customers. Its potential impact on the employees will be discussed in Chapter 8.

Of course, numerous examples of the successful internationalization of service delivery exist, for example, in fields such as accounting, architecture, healthcare and education. In the last of these, it is easy to see how provision of services internationally has become highly developed and that higher education (HE), whilst being a form of IB itself, constitutes both a consequence and a driver of internationalization and the globalization of business activities. As a form of IB, having advantages of English as a primary language, universities in the USA, the UK and Australia have been at the forefront of developments. They have not achieved a monopoly, however, as HE institutions in other, non-English speaking countries have also been active in offering English-language taught programmes aimed at the international student market. International HE has developed on a large scale through various forms, starting with the basic 'import' of undergraduate students to English-speaking countries from other parts of the world. These students can be seen as examples of 'clients' travelling internationally in order to receive the educational 'service'. As the HE business has matured and as the 'exporting' countries build up their reserves of graduates, we have witnessed a degree of movement by some countries from exporting students to 'importing' the provision of education. Other than basic import/ export activities, approaches to HE internationalization include examples of strategic alliances, franchising, joint ventures and foreign direct investment. These can be observed, respectively, in the form of collaborative agreements between institutions, the granting of rights to award degrees in the name of a foreign institution, the establishment of joint ventures such as the China Europe International Business School (CEIBS) and Australian RMIT University's development of a campus in Vietnam.

The above examples show how HE delivery has developed as a form of IB service provision. However, HE is more than a mere supplier of services, but also has an impact upon the formation of future managers and other organizational practitioners, and as such influences the nature of contemporary international business. In recent times, with the expansion of business and management education at a global level, the ubiquitous MBA qualification has grown to become both the core service offering of an internationalized higher education industry and a necessary 'badge of office' for the aspiring senior manager who seeks employment mobility in the international business arena. Whilst there is some variety in the service offerings of individual institutions, there are common expectations about the content of courses, the models of business that are presented, and the terminology conveyed to students. In addition, some critics have pointed to the dominance of

Anglo-American preconceptions of what constitutes 'good' business practice.

Altogether, service delivery at an international level covers a wide range of activities. It shares some elements of its financial and institutional order with other forms of IB, but raises particular issues of culture, language and skills transfer, to which we will return in Chapter 8.

conclusion

In this chapter, we have addressed a number of areas typically classified as aspects of 'international management'. These have included R&D, marketing, logistics and supply chain management, and issues involved in service delivery at an international level. In our discussion, we have attempted to point out that what companies do within these fields of activity does not only impact on their own position in the market, but also has implications for those outside the organization. In some cases, these implications are far from positive. In particular, in considering R&D, we have highlighted how the commonly followed logic of focusing on low-risk and high-return developments has created a situation where insufficient investment is made in research aimed at developing medicines that would help address some of the health problems of populations in third world countries.

With regard to international marketing, we have sought to problematize the assumption about the fulfilment of consumer needs by companies' products and services. Specifically, we have pointed to some examples of products that are marketed internationally and that bring about outcomes that are potentially or actually detrimental to the health of those who consume them. As far as the field of logistics and supply chain management is concerned, we have drawn our readers' attention to the unequal power relations underpinning the development of global supply chains. These result in a situation of dependency of workers in low-cost locations upon the insecure conditions of employment by

MNEs. This is true not only in the case of the manufacture of tangible products, but also of service delivery, as exemplified in industries such as call centres or data-processing centres. Moreover, we have raised the question of the negative consequences for the natural environment stemming from global logistics activities.

In the next chapter, we continue our discussion of international management and its broader impacts by turning to the topics of finance, accounting and governance.

7

Finance, Accounting and Governance

Tax is the foundation of good government and a key to the wealth or poverty of nations. Yet it is under attack.

Tax Justice Network

introduction

Organizations that are involved in contemporary IB are frequently transnational in nature, having operating bases in multiple countries, and, as such, they engage in intra-organizational transactions between their own business units and subsidiaries, as well as in exchange with other organizations. In this chapter, we will outline the various factors that impact organizations' decision making on the financial aspects of international operations and investment, along with issues relating to international taxation and the efforts of businesses to minimize their global tax liabilities. We will consider conflicts inherent in the nature of financial management and accounting when the different interests of a range of global stakeholders are taken into account. Finally, we will discuss issues of governance of organizations engaging in IB.

the international firm and its relationship with its subsidiaries

According to Czinkota et al. (2005), firms engaging in international business seek to balance three financial goals, namely, to maximize their overall earnings after the deduction of tax, to minimize their effective global tax liability, and to optimize the location of their income, cash flows and available funds. We will look at what actions are commonly taken by MNEs as they address these three goals, and what implications they have for stakeholders other than organizations' managers and shareholders.

One of the major areas that permit scope for MNEs to achieve their desired international financial goals lies in the structuring and management of relationships between the parent company and its subsidiaries, as well as between subsidiaries across the world. Drawing upon Perlmutter's (1969) categories, three generic strategies for organizing the parent/subsidiary relationship can be classified, as follows: polycentric, ethnocentric and geocentric.

The first of these is the most decentralized in that financial decisions are taken to a large extent at the level of the subsidiary. The performance of each subsidiary is assessed against that of other firms operating in the same market environment, and its financial statements are prepared in accordance with generally accepted accounting principles of both the subsidiary's and the parent company's home countries.

The ethnocentric approach, on the other hand, involves centralization of the management functions of the MNE. In relation to finance, this translates into the integration of the financial planning and control of subsidiary operations into the parent company's systems and treats the subsidiaries as mere extensions of the main business.

The geocentric solution is an attempt to exploit the advantages and avoid the pitfalls of each of the first two approaches in relation to individual markets. The decision regarding which subsidiaries should be managed using the polycentric versus the ethnocentric model is based upon the parent company's judgement in relation to the relative suitability of one or the other for each subsidiary's market. Whilst a more detailed discussion of the financial management aspect of the relationship between the parent company and its subsidiaries is beyond the scope of our discussion here, those of you interested in this topic may wish to read further (e.g. Czinkota et al., 2005; Rugman and Collinson, 2006).

▓▓▓▓ global cash management and the use of transfer pricing

Together with determining the relationship between the parent company and its subsidiaries, international financial management encompasses decisions regarding global cash management. A key cash management issue that an international firm needs to address relates to the total amount of cash it holds globally. With a number of separate subsidiaries across the world, it might seem logical that each would hold its own funds to meet its own transactional needs in its individual market. However, from the MNE's financial management point of view, this represents an over-provision of resources, increasing the company's overall operating costs. As large companies within a single country will generally centralize their key management functions, so MNEs seek to do the same at a global level. Of course, due to the greater complexity and limitations of transferring funds internationally, compared to within national boundaries, the scope for cash management centralization is lower in the case of an MNE. In addition, whilst central control may be seen as desirable by corporate headquarters, to the subsidiaries, it may represent a restriction on autonomy and on the ability to manage their own performance.

There are a number of strategies that MNEs tend to employ in order to manage their internal flows of funds. These are subject to varying degrees of control and regulation within different country financial regimes. One of the ways in which funds are managed is through 'multilateral netting', where it is legally permitted. In a situation where multiple business units of a given MNE undertake a large amount of intra-company transactions with one another, they will in theory owe money to each other in relation to every one of these. The use of multilateral netting enables the cumulative sums due to be balanced out amongst the subsidiaries, such that only the remaining amount left after netting needs to be transferred between accounts.

Another strategy that may be applied to global cash flow management is that of 'internal lending' between business units, whereby one unit reduces its taxable income through lending money to another at a low interest rate. At the same time, the borrowing unit obtains necessary capital investment at a lower rate of interest than would be charged by an external lending institution. Whilst, from the viewpoint of the MNE and its stockholders, this is seen as an advantageous business practice, it implicitly assumes that it is not problematic that the amount of tax that is 'saved' for the company will simultaneously represent a 'loss' of taxation revenue for the relevant countries.

MNEs can adopt similar strategies in relation to the internal transfer of payments for products, components or services provided by one subsidiary or the parent to another business unit. Where parts of the MNE pay the same rate for such goods or services as would be charged to an external customer, the overall level of taxation due is not affected. However, this is not always the case, since 'transfer pricing' strategies are often adopted by MNEs in order to assist them in meeting their goals of maximizing overall profitability, minimizing global tax liabilities, or facilitating the transfer of funds between business units. In such circumstances, the price paid may bear little or no relation to the market value of the particular commodity or service. Additionally, in a situation where more than half of world trade takes place within corporations rather than between them and their external customers (Tax Justice Network, 2005), there may well be no 'market price' for many of the goods and services in question.

In determining the level of prices in such intra-company transactions, the general logic is to create a situation where taxable income is moved from countries with higher tax rates to those characterized by lower ones. In this way, the firm adds to its earnings the difference between the amount of tax that would have had to be paid if transfer pricing had not taken place and the amount of tax actually paid following the intra-company trade and the tax-reducing price-setting techniques accompanying it. An illustration of the extent to which manipulation of prices set for internal exports and imports can be used to distort the MNE's balance sheet, and hence its tax liabilities, is provided by Sikka

(2003), who outlines how a US multinational company will, for
example, import plastic buckets from its Czech subsidiary at a
price of $973 each, fence posts from Canada at $1,853, or a
ballpoint pen from Trinidad for $8,500. At the same time, it
will export bulldozers to Venezuela at a unit price of $388, and
missile and rocket launchers to Israel for just $52 each. He
explains that:

> Such practices make a dramatic difference to tax yields. The UK sub-
> sidiary of a multinational company constructs a bulldozer at a cost of
> £27,000 but sells it for £300 to another subsidiary in the same group
> of companies based, say, in Venezuela, which then sells it on for its
> market price of £60,000. For tax purposes, the UK subsidiary could
> claim a loss of £26,700 and pay no corporation tax, even though the
> group made a global profit of £33,000. That profit is generated by
> using British infrastructure, but is recorded in another country with a
> more favourable fiscal regime. (Sikka, 2003)

The issue of transfer pricing has caused 'sleepless nights' (*Economist*,
2007) for taxmen the world over, and Peter Schott of Yale School
of Management estimated that it costs the US Internal Revenue
Service (IRS) between $5.5 billion and $30 billion each year in lost
revenue (*Economist*, 2007). However, as noted in *The Economist*,
tax authorities are becoming more aggressive in seeking to overcome transfer pricing anomalies and it records that in 2006, international pharmaceutical giant GlaxoSmithKline settled a transfer
pricing dispute with the IRS that had lasted 16 years with a payment
of $3 billion. This shows that, increasingly, it is becoming obvious for
governments that the MNEs' drive towards profit-maximization
may have a negative impact on a country's budget and on its ability to provide public goods for its citizens.

international taxation and issues of tax havens

The example of transfer pricing depicts one of the ways in which
MNEs take account of differences in tax regimes between countries,
based upon variations in taxation rates. Another common tax

avoidance strategy involves exploitation of 'tax havens', that is countries that have particularly low tax rates and that are regarded as 'hospitable to business'. As the Tax Justice Network (2007: 1) points out, 'while almost any jurisdiction can have some tax haven … features, a smaller number are usually identified as "pure" tax havens. … The central feature of a haven is that its laws and other measures can be used to evade or avoid the tax laws or regulations of other jurisdictions.' The use of tax havens is often pursued by MNEs in conjunction with transfer pricing, whereby they arrange the sale of products or services at a very low price from one subsidiary to another located in a tax haven, which then sells on to yet another subsidiary at a very high price. In this way, the profit occurs in the tax haven country and, as such, is subject to the lowest possible level of taxation – in some cases, no taxation at all. Tax havens not only enable companies to pursue a strategy of tax minimization but, since they generally lack transparency in how their legislative, judicial and administrative functions operate, they are also used as a means of hiding information about business transactions and actual profit levels.

Some commentators (e.g. Tax Justice Network, 2005) discuss how the use of tax havens, with their lack of transparency about the nature of business that takes place within and between them, creates opportunities for the concealment of funds generated from activities that are illegal in most countries, such as drug trafficking, money laundering and people trafficking. This refers, in particular, to situations in which more than one tax haven location is employed, and where the identities of individuals are covered up by the use of nominee names and by vesting company ownership in trusts. Nominee names are persons who are not directly involved in the company's operations, but who, for a fee, are willing to say that they are a director of a tax haven company. Trusts are third-party entities, usually with nominee directors and often set up in a different tax haven, which hold legal ownership of the company in question. As a result of arrangements involving multiple tax havens, nominee names and trusts, it becomes very difficult, if not impossible, to establish what business transactions are taking place and who is benefiting from them. If, as a reader, you are confused by this explanation, you will see how it is that:

> tax haven activity appears to take place nowhere. Which means it is accountable to no one, and has no duty to report anything because it can deny it is anywhere. In the secretive, parallel universe of tax havens, structures can be set up to carry out real functions in the real world but without any requirement for a transparent legal presence that confirms their existence or the nature of their activities. (Tax Justice Network, 2005: 27)

There is, however, some movement towards changing the rules of the game in relation to companies' use of tax havens. At the time of writing, US presidential candidate Barack Obama is one of three American senators who have introduced the Stop Tax Haven Abuse Act, claiming that tax havens cost the US economy $100 billion per year. In the UK, there is a proposal to offer an amnesty to those who have used tax havens in order to avoid their UK tax liabilities. These moves prompt consideration of where the fine line exists between tax minimization and tax avoidance, between what is legal or illegal, and what is considered ethical.

country-specific frameworks and financial risk management

In addition to considerations of taxation, there are a number of other factors that will influence organizations' financial decision making in the context of IB. These include issues of currency stability and the legislative frameworks that enable or constrain fund transfer by international firms. Whilst businesses may seek to maximize the gains from exploiting low tax regimes, they also have to be wary of fluctuations in the value of currencies in which they do business. For example, a firm may be based in the United States and conduct most of its business in US dollars, but also have an operating subsidiary in a country that has a currency that fluctuates widely in value relative to the dollar. Even if this country has a tax regime with lower rates than the USA, the risks presented by the possibility of a drastic fall in the value of the currency of the country will more than likely drive the firm to seek to transfer funds out at the earliest opportunity when the exchange rate is beneficial for this. However, the firm's ability to conduct this transfer may be restricted by legislation within the country that makes it difficult, or impossible, to repatriate earnings to the home country.

Whilst much of the discourse on globalization gives the impression that MNEs today operate freely at a global level, with the ability to move their operations, investments and earnings between nations at will, this is not necessarily the case. Country governments are still important players in setting rules that determine the extent to which capital is mobile across the globe. In fact, the vast majority of less developed economies, as well as many of the developed ones, impose restrictions on funds outflows. For example, the People's Republic of China (PRC) has historically had one of the most restrictive financial regimes, in terms of limiting the possibility for outward funds transfer. Whilst there is some evidence of a relaxation of the previous regime since China's accession to the World Trade Organization (WTO), in order to allow some amount of outward flow of funds, both for individuals and firms, it is not at all clear that these changes will satisfy the expectations of today's MNEs. This does not mean that international companies do not enter the Chinese market, which has been one of the fastest-growing economies in the last decade. However, they use a number of financial strategies in order to minimize the risks and to ease their global fund transfer processes.

One of these is the use of 'fronting loans', which involves the employment of a third-party financial institution in the process of financing operations in a country with currency transfer restrictions. This arrangement requires the parent to deposit an amount of capital in its home country, but with an international bank that has a strong presence in, say, China. The Chinese subsidiary of the bank then provides a loan in this amount to the company's operation in PRC. In effect, the organization funds its PRC business unit on the basis of a debt to the bank, to be repaid with interest from profits earned in China. At the same time, it holds a positive balance of funds on deposit in its home country. In this way, it reduces its exposure to risk and to currency transfer restrictions since its own movement of monies takes place within and not across national boundaries.

Other approaches to managing risks related to international transactions refer to dealing with three major types of exchange risk, namely, transaction risk, translation risk (or accounting risk) and economic risk. A detailed explanation of these would require more space than we can dedicate to it in this short book, and therefore we refer our readers to sources that deal with the topic of currency exchange risks in a comprehensive manner (e.g. Eun and Resnick, 2006).

international finance and investment

To this point in the chapter, we have considered international financial management in relation to primarily intra-organizational issues, noting that the majority of IB transactions take place within this arena. We now turn our attention to financial issues that impact on firms seeking to undertake trade with, or investment in, other countries where they are not themselves already established. Here, compared to setting up new activities within the home country, companies must take account of a broader range of factors specific to the intended host country. In addition to the previously discussed foreign exchange and taxation issues, the potential impact of the overall macro-economic and political environment needs to be considered. As governments seek to encourage foreign companies to invest in their countries, they may offer a range of financial incentives to the inward investors in order to attract them, but may also place conditions upon the way in which the companies can operate if they want to take advantage of the market. Government strategies for promoting 'foreign direct investment' (FDI) might include the provision of low interest loans, tax exemptions or tax 'holidays', or subsidies for the acquisition of capital plant and equipment.

Whilst it is common to find the provision of financial incentives for FDI, some countries may place restrictions on the ownership of assets by foreign enterprises, both as a general principle or as a condition of receipt of these incentives. Additionally, the host country may place requirements on how the business can be structured, including a need to employ certain numbers of local staff, to purchase certain supplies, components or services in the local market, or to license technologies at the local level. In this way, governments attempt to ensure that the FDI results in positive outcomes for the host country's economy and society, which, as we discussed in Chapter 3, is not always the case.

In order to appraise the viability of foreign investments, firms will generally apply a quantitative analysis based upon the net present value (NPV) of combined income and outgoings projections over a specific investment period. The term 'net present value' refers to projected future earnings from the project, where the value of these earnings is discounted by taking away the amount of interest that the investment capital used to fund the project might have earned if invested in other ways. The organization must take account of this 'lost' earning potential from interest, the 'opportunity cost' of the investment. The fine detail of NPV calculation is beyond the scope of this work, but suffice it to say that organizations will look favourably upon investment opportunities which show a positive NPV reconciliation of projected incomings and outgoings, that is the overall earnings less expenses, when discounted to the present day, are greater than the interest that could be earned from an alternative investment.

When firms enter the international market and seek to do business with companies in other countries, there may be initial concerns about issues of financial trust. In order to overcome these, companies entering into international contracts for the supply of goods will often draw upon the use of a 'letter of credit' to guarantee the financial credibility of the customer. This arrangement involves the customer organization demonstrating to its bank that it has sufficient funds to cover the contract price. The bank will then pass this letter to the supplier's bank. Whilst there are some variations in the detail of the process, the key point is that, at the end of the transaction, the supplier draws payment from the bank that has provided the guarantee, not from the customer itself. It is up to the customer's bank to ensure that it recoups the contract amount.

Having discussed the many ways in which financial transactions can be structured, we must point out that, in the present day, many international trade exchanges do not involve the transfer of currency. Throughout history, barter has been widely employed as a means of conducting trade, as individuals and communities have shared their own surplus production of goods and materials with others in exchange for the supply to them of other commodities which they lack. In the contemporary world of IB, the exchange of goods, services, technologies and even ideas through the process of 'countertrade' is common practice. Often, this takes place not between pairs of organizations, but at the level of the country. The reasons for adopting a countertrade approach can be many, ranging from a desire to avoid currency transfer or the non-convertibility of a currency, to a wish to attain strategic advantage over a competing supplier.

As with other forms of financial exchange, there are a variety of different types of countertrade but, in general, they involve the transfer of an agreed quantity of item X from country A to country B, in return for the reciprocal supply of a quantity of item Y from country B to country A. In the recent past, countertrade has been used by a number of governments as a means of procuring military equipment, such as fighter aircraft or missile defence systems. In the overall pattern of contemporary exchange at a global level, the items traded may range from tea or rice to aircraft or locomotives, and from the construction of transport infrastructure to the supply of gas or electricity. One of the most highly publicized examples of countertrade in recent times involved PepsiCo's dealings with the former Soviet Union, where it first entered into an exchange of Pepsi-Cola syrup for Stolichnaya Vodka and later accepted '17 submarines, a cruiser, a frigate, and a destroyer in payment for Pepsi products. In turn, this rag tag fleet of 20 naval vessels [was to] be sold for scrap steel, thereby paying for Pepsi products being moved to the Soviet Union' (West, 1996).

accounting conventions and financial reporting

The preparation of financial reports is an activity that is common to organizations, both domestically and internationally. The actual content of the reports reflects the nature of the organization and the transactions it undertakes, and must also comply with the requirements of the accounting system, or systems, under which it operates. Traditionally, these systems have been developed at a national level by the relevant regulatory bodies. The nature of these systems is grounded in the legal framework of individual countries. Broadly speaking, there are two generic approaches to financial regulation: rule-based and principle-based approaches. In the first, accounting practices are determined by law and are codified. In the second, the practices are laid out by the professional body in accounting and set out in terms of a general framework of compliance.

In the context of IB, MNEs and international firms must comply with the accounting and financial reporting practices of the various countries within which they operate. These practices will not only incorporate different principles in accordance with the various frameworks, but are also likely to involve reporting in a range of different currencies. For example, an MNE with its headquarters in France and subsidiaries across multiple countries will be required to produce separate financial reports for each of the subsidiaries within the countries where they are based. At the same time, the organization is legally required to produce consolidated accounts for the entire business in France. Moreover, if, for example, the MNE is listed not only on the Paris Bourse but also on the New York Stock Exchange (NYSE), it will have to produce further reports in accordance with the US Securities and Exchange Commission (SEC) rules. The French reports will need to be presented in euros, those for the NYSE in US dollars, whilst other currencies may be required in the subsidiaries' separate markets. The parent company faces choices about whether to require the subsidiaries to report to it in euros, US dollars, or in their own currency. Depending upon fluctuating exchange rates, the final choice may result in inflating or depressing the value of the firm's assets or liabilities.

Together with drives for economic integration, as outlined in Part II, and the increasing power of MNEs as actors within the global economy, recent years have seen developments towards the harmonization of accounting and financial reporting, auditing and stock exchange standards. An important role within these efforts has been played by organizations such as the International Accounting Standards Board (IASB), the International Auditing and Assurance Standards Board (IAASB), and the International Organization of Securities Commission (IOSCO), supported by national standard setters. In addition, the European Union has developed its own set of accounting standards to be applied within member states. The major players in IB generally view the outputs of these organizations as leading to an improvement in terms of levels of disclosure and transparency, and to a reduction in 'dubious' practices. From the point of view of MNEs, harmonization initiatives are a positive phenomenon as they make their business easier to coordinate globally and contribute to lowering their costs through simplifying their reporting processes. For investors, the transparency and comparability achieved through harmonization has made it easier for them to make investment decisions. Likewise, as harmonized standards become more widely used, and in the process of development become more complex, they are considered to reduce the likelihood of accounting scandals (such as Enron, Parmalat and Worldcom), or of a recurrence of economic problems like those of South East Asian countries in the 1990s, which were seen by some as being compounded by lack of transparency in accounting procedures.

However, there have also been critical voices pointing to the fact that the process of internationalization of accounting standards is not one that involves the integration of accounting principles and rules from a variety of national accounting systems. Rather, it is based upon the spread of standards originating within western accounting practices, which might not be appropriate for organizations operating within environments substantially different from, say, the UK. Further, it is generally perceived that whilst the United States is broadly in favour of harmonization, it would like to see this happening in line with American standards, which are considered to be more rigid and prescriptive than those set out by the IASB. A critical examination of the political interests and power structures underpinning the standardization of accounting practices across countries has led Sikka (2007: 1) to describe them as 'colonialism in another guise, allowing tax avoidance while foisting failed practices without oversight or democratic control'.

governance and accountability

In recent years, much attention has been focused on the issue of 'corporate governance', the term that defines the relationship between various stakeholders and that sets the framework for control and strategic direction of the organization. The governance structure of an organization is central to its very being and is frequently determined by the legal framework of the country in which it is registered. As such, it is generally seen as offering a high degree of assurance and consistency in relation to the propriety and legality of its management. In addition, the requirement for independent audit of the company accounts each year is viewed as providing a check on this for the financial shareholders. The key purpose of structures of governance is to provide transparency of the company's operations and financial results.

In the Anglo-American business world, the central tenet of corporate governance is that of 'outsider control', which prioritizes the financial interests of the shareholders and places responsibility for this with management. Moreover, it assumes the existence of a capital market in which shares are bought and sold by investors. The framework of corporate governance is provided by the state within its legal system. Within this system, the top management of the company is accountable to the board of directors, whilst the board is accountable to shareholders. In addition, the governance of organizations is overseen by a range of governmental and non-governmental bodies. A further measure of control over public companies is provided, whereby they must submit their annual reports to independent external audit. The auditors must not only check the accuracy of the financial reports, but must also certify that the firm has complied with all necessary statutes.

At an international level, the Organization for Economic Cooperation and Development (OECD, 2004) has set out *Principles of Corporate Governance*. The document stresses that corporate governance is about the timely and accurate disclosure of company information and the transparency of management decision making. The OECD principles are constructed around the primacy of the financial shareholders and the protection of their rights. They require the equitable treatment of all shareholders, including institutional investors, minority shareholders and non-national shareholders. Beyond the concerns of those with financial interests, the document also refers to the rights of stakeholders, as established in law or through agreements with the firm. The level to which non-shareholder stakeholders have rights over the activities of an organization varies from country to country and is subject to change over time. In Germany, for example, in businesses with more than five employees there is a statutory requirement for them to establish a 'workers' council'. This council must then be consulted about certain management decisions before implementation. Other countries offer no such statutory employee involvement.

The separation of ownership from management, characteristic of the Anglo-American public company environment, does not apply to the same extent in all markets. In Latin America, for example, there is a strong tradition of family ownership and involvement in businesses and hence, even in large companies, the distinction between ownership and management might not be so clear. In Japan, on the other hand, the second half of the twentieth century saw the emergence of the large *keiretsu*, a conglomerate of multi-industry businesses that is owned by one of the major banks, such as Bank of Tokyo-Mitsubishi UFJ or Sumitomo Mitsui Bank.

Despite the intent of corporate governance to protect the interests of shareholders and stakeholders outside the firm, recent years have seen a number of high-profile failures, brought about by the greed and lack of morality of individuals. The most notable of these was the collapse of Enron, the US energy giant in 2001, where directors systematically set out to deceive investors, employees and the public at large. They used a number of offshore companies and bogus transactions between different entities in order to build a picture of growth and profitability when, in fact, the businesses were accumulating high losses. As the share price rose, these directors divested themselves of their stock, earning vast amounts. As the price began to fall, they maintained their story of confidence and persuaded investors to continue to pour money into a failing enterprise. When the scandal was finally revealed, the aftermath led not only to the conviction and jailing of the former Chairman, Kenneth Lay, and the CEO, Jeffrey Skilling, but also to the collapse of the firm's auditors Arthur Andersen, which had been one of the 'big five' global accounting firms, now reduced to the 'big four'. Enron was not the only such governance failure to hit the headlines, and the scandals of US Worldcom and Italian Parmalat have drawn media attention and generated calls for tighter regulation and control. In the USA, the response was to impose tighter regulatory control over companies through the provisions of the Sarbanes–Oxley Act, which places new responsibilities on company CEOs, boards and auditors, and prohibits company lending to its officers and directors. In Europe, the European Commission delegated responsibility for tightening procedures to individual member states, following which country governments and professional bodies introduced new regulations and codes on corporate governance.

At the present time, however, questions remain about overall issues of accountability, taxation and governance across the globe and, beyond the level of legitimate businesses and their tax minimization or tax avoidance strategies, there are broader concerns about the use of offshoring and tax havens in order to launder the proceeds of drug and people trafficking, and to raise funds for terrorist activities.

alternative models of finance and investment

In the wake of corporate scandals such as Enron and Worldcom, and with acceptance of evidence of global warming and environmental degradation, there has been growing pressure from some financial stakeholders for a reassessment of the myopic focus on profits. In addition, despite the dominant role of Anglo-American standards in areas such as accounting and finance, there is increasing awareness of and interest in alternative approaches, such as ethical banking. Amongst financial institutions there are businesses, such as the Ecology Building Society and the Cooperative Bank in the UK, that offer financial services based upon ecological criteria or that renounce investment in the arms industry. There is also a growing interest in Islamic banking. Since its formation in 1975, the Dubai Islamic Bank has developed around Shari'ah principles of finance and now provides investment funding at a global level. As Islamic banking develops to become one of the fastest-growing areas in international finance, the major global players in banking, such as CitiBank, HSBC and National Australia Bank, have developed divisions or offerings that specifically target the Islamic market through compliance with these principles (Hell, 2006).

Another model of finance that is aimed specifically at entrepreneurs in developing economies is 'microfinance' and, at the present time, major banking corporations are targeting prospective customers in developing countries with new offerings (e.g. Allianz, 2007). These are advertised as offering access to start-up funds for potential entrepreneurs who otherwise would not have an opportunity to secure capital. However, the concept of microfinance has been criticized on several points. To some, it represents a good idea but is too limited in its outreach; to others, it fails to address structural problems of poor governance and lack of accountability in developing countries. In addition, some consider it ethically dubious to lend to the poor rather than giving.

conclusion

In this chapter, we have sought to offer an overview of financial and accounting frameworks, and their implications for the range of entities that have an interest in these at a global level. In the space of this short book, we have been able to cover only the basics of the vast range of different aspects of these topics. In relation to financial management, we have focused primarily on issues of relevance to large commercial organizations operating in many countries, and we have provided some examples of the practices they engage in when managing their finances. We have had to be selective in deciding which areas of international financial management we address, and have chosen to draw particular attention to those aspects that are not necessarily widely covered in mainstream IB texts, for example, issues of transfer pricing, the use of tax havens, and the possibilities of these being used as a means of fronting illegal activities. This has allowed us to point to the inherent conflict between the interests of countries and MNEs in relation to taxation issues.

As far as international accounting is concerned, in this chapter we have discussed recent initiatives aimed at the standardization of accounting and financial reporting across nations. Those who support these moves point to the advantages for firms and international investors of greater comparability between financial reports prepared in accordance with rules of different countries, along with higher levels of transparency for governments and other bodies. We have also addressed the issue of corporate governance and its importance in the light of recent accounting scandals.

In concluding our discussion of international financial management, accounting and governance, we would like to point out that the topics discussed here are relevant not only to companies and governments as actors in IB. Through their impact on country economies and budgets, they affect individuals across societies. For example, the influence of practices of transfer pricing and the use of tax havens will be felt on levels of social benefits derived from taxation, such as retirement pensions, education and health-care. On the other hand, affected individuals may also be investors with an interest in maximizing their return on investment, and so possibly being in favour of tax minimization or avoidance. Finally, we have pointed to some of the alternative models of finance that are of interest in the contemporary world.

As we have hopefully shown, within contemporary IB, there is a complex network of interdependencies between different stake-holders. These interdependencies transcend national boundaries and can be understood only partially when issues of international finance, accounting and governance are considered solely from the perspective of MNEs. Therefore, as in the rest of this book, we would like to encourage you to think about them from the point of view of the widest possible range of parties involved in and affected by them.

8

Managing People in the International Arena

We not only have targets, we grade agents into three categories: A – Excellent, B – Satisfactory and C – Not meeting standards. With Personal Improvement Plans, the Cs are taken out, and if they do not become As or Bs after a short time, then unfortunately they have to go.

Manager of a call centre in Mumbai
(cited in Taylor and Bain, 2005)

introduction

The example of Norwich Union's transfer of work from the UK to India (see Chapter 6) is grounded in the premise that IT is the major source of advantage in international service delivery. In support of this approach, the company's Executive Chairman stated that, 'As you use more technology, you need fewer people'. In contrast to this organization's downplaying of the significance of the human element, one academic study from 2002 (Colman, 2002, cited in Hill, 2007: 619) argued that human resources constitutes one of the weakest performance areas of firms engaging in international business and suggested that more effective human resource management (HRM) practices might offer substantive performance benefits for companies. We would argue that discussion of international HRM should also take account of ways in which different HRM strategies impact the very subject of HRM theory and practice, that is people. Whilst much of the mainstream literature on managing people in the IB arena is directed at HRM practices for selection, training and development, and compensation of ex-patriot managers working for MNEs, we see that there is a range of broader issues that are relevant to critical discussion of the IB field. In particular, we believe in the need to move beyond the understanding of human resources in IB as managers of companies, to include the millions of workers employed by firms operating internationally or globally, and their subcontractors. Moreover, we wish to reflect upon and challenge the assumptions behind the theoretical frameworks and practices typically recommended for use in the area of HRM. To this end, we address the concepts of cultural differences and diversity, HR policies and practices in international organizations, and issues of international labour relations.

culture, organization and society

In our view, discussion of the management of people in the international arena requires consideration of the notion of 'culture'. There are multiple intellectual frames for understanding culture. For example, the term tends to be considered in relation both to the organization and to the countries in which it operates. Second, culture can be perceived from either an instrumentalist perspective, as some 'thing' that can be managed, or in a non-instrumentalist way, as an influencing factor to be acknowledged and accommodated. Moreover, cultural differences can be seen either as a 'problem' to be overcome, or as a learning opportunity that provides access to new forms of knowledge and understanding. Notwithstanding the differences that characterize extant approaches to the subject of culture and cultural difference in an international context, the literature highlights some common features amongst the various conceptualizations of culture.

Culture is generally seen as comprising a set of shared values, beliefs and assumptions that guide the thinking of individuals and encapsulate norms of behaviour within a group. Some texts address the concept at a level of national or organizational culture and might be read as implying an overriding homogeneity of these traits. In particular, in the field of international management, there is an emphasis on defining and recognizing the existence of cultural differences between nations. It is understood that an international organization will typically employ staff from different cultural backgrounds, and that the realization of the values and beliefs that underpin actions of international staff members is essential for effective management. Within the literature on managing across cultures, amongst frequently referenced works are those of Geert Hofstede (1984), whose 'dimensions' of national culture are often read as defining characteristics of specific countries. Hofstede initially undertook empirical research within IBM across arout 70 countries in the period from 1967 to 1973 and, from his survey data for the 40 largest countries he identified four dimensions for classification of national cultures: power distance, uncertainty avoidance, individualism versus collectivism, and masculinity versus femininity.

The first dimension relates to the extent to which societies are characterized by either high levels of hierarchy and power inequalities, or by flatter structures and more equal power relations. Uncertainty avoidance is a measure of the extent to which people are comfortable to live with ambiguity and a willingness to take risks, or seek clarity of purpose within a clear structure. The third dimension concerns the relationship between the individual and the group, and the extent to which personal achievement is prioritized over the good of society as a whole. The final dimension is not a measure of gender *per se*, but concerns the extent to which 'masculine' traits of assertiveness, competitiveness and material success dominate, or to which 'softer' feminine concerns for societal and environmental issues are exhibited. Hofstede's conceptualization of culture was further developed in conjunction with Bond (Hofstede and Bond, 1988), by introducing the additional dimension of 'Confucian dynamism'. This dimension relates to the extent to which societies adopt either a long-term or short-term outlook.

Whilst Hofstede's work is widely used as a source for discussion of 'how to' manage across cultures, it has been criticized on a number of counts (e.g. McSweeney, 2002). These refer to the narrowness of the organizational and national settings of the study, its conduct by western researchers, the methodology used for data collection and analysis, and its generalization and clustering of 'national' cultures. In addition, it is now pointed out that the study was undertaken in an historical context that pre-dated the collapse of the Soviet bloc, the opening up of China to international business, and the development of global communications networks. Whilst the severest critics would discount the work on these bases, Hofstede's framework is still applied in the field of cross-cultural management and has been built upon and expanded by other researchers, such as House et al. (2004). We would suggest that, whether or not one agrees with Hofstede's approach, his contribution needs to be recognized as drawing our attention to issues of cultural difference and as inspiring further work in this area.

Another framework that deals with cultural difference is that of Hall and Hall (1990), who highlight the importance of context in determining the meaning ascribed to communication. They draw a distinction between 'high-context' and 'low-context' cultures. In the former, the meaning of communication needs to be interpreted in relation to both the textual content and the social context in which it takes place. In the latter, on the other hand, meaning is explicitly expressed through the words alone. Japan is usually cited as a high-context society, whereas the USA is seen as low-context. As with Hofstede's work, Hall and Hall's text should be read as offering guidance rather than the 'truth' about cultural differences. In the IB literature, use of both Hofstede's and Hall and Hall's frameworks is based upon the assumption that, following the identification of cultural differences between individuals of different nationalities, it becomes possible to better manage these individuals as employees, customers or as other parties with which the international organization interacts.

The approaches that are exemplified in the works of Hofstede, House et al., and Hall and Hall are rooted in an anthropological conceptualization of culture, where emphasis is placed on single-country cultural characteristics and on comparisons between specific national cultures. They do not, for example, raise questions about cultural differences within nations as well as changes in national cultures over time. Taking account of the breakdown of national boundaries, the increasing mobility of people, and the development of global communications networks, Holden (2002: 284) takes 'a few tentative steps' towards a re-definition of cultural difference as a potential organizational resource with knowledge generation capabilities, rather than as 'a nuisance at best and often a disaster' (Hofstede, 1997: 10). In a similar vein, Magala (2005) draws attention to the fact that contemporary international management recognizes the existence of cultural diversity within organizations and sees it as requiring managerial attention in terms of addressing issues of gender, age, education, ethnicity, sexuality and religion. As such, more contemporary perspectives on managing culture in organizations, including international firms, are set within the context of 'diversity management'. Here, differences between individuals are not discussed exclusively from the point of view of national culture, but with regard for these other characteristics. In this way, our consideration of culture is moved beyond it being seen as a unifying nationality-based framework and as a 'problem' to be overcome, to open up our thinking to both the complex challenges and the opportunities presented by cultural diversity. We believe that culture, both at a national and an organizational level, must not be seen as solid and monolithic and able to be designed or controlled through the application of managerial processes. Rather, it should be seen as fluid and diverse, and thereby as both influencing and being influenced by these processes.

In relation to the explicit consideration of culture in the mainstream IB literature, there are two critical issues that we should consider. First, as Tipton (2008) has pointed out, these texts often contain assertions about cultural traits that are ill-founded, such as his example of the perpetuated myth that 'thumbs-up is a rude gesture in Australia'. In addition to the explicit errors, there is also an implicit assumption in the IB literature that all other cultures are, or should be, compared to that of the United States. The case studies of organizations and their internationalization are dominated by tales of US firms, and the pervading values and norms of international management throughout the discourse are those of the manager in such organizations.

staffing policy and HR practices in the international organization

The international organization faces choices regarding who to employ in its worldwide operations and within the separate country markets in which it does business. In relation to the cultural background of recruited management staff members, three general approaches can be identified (Hill, 2007): ethnocentric, polycentric and geocentric. The first of these relates to a policy of employing home-country nationals in key management positions in all markets. This approach was popular amongst firms that sought to maintain a strong identity and company focus. The popularity of the ethnocentric approach has waned in response to issues of cultural myopia and the lack of career development opportunities for host country staff. The second approach is one of employing host country staff in senior posts. Here, from the point of view of the organization's top management, there are the advantages of local knowledge, but there may be barriers to wider communication and transfer within the firm, due to language and other differences. The geocentric approach, which can be related to identification with cultural diversity, involves the firm in selecting the best possible people for all management positions across the organization, regardless of nationality. It is worth noting that there is an underlying assumption that, no matter which of these three approaches is adopted, profit and other benefits to the firm are prioritized over whatever advantages and disadvantages might accrue to the individual and to the society in which the company operates. In the field of healthcare in the UK, for example, a shortage of suitably qualified staff has led to the active recruitment of nursing and other staff from Africa, without regard for the resultant chronic shortage of trained staff to provide an adequate level of care and, in countries such as Malawi, with their own problems of endemic HIV and malaria.

Beyond nationality, the reality of staffing decisions within firms requires a consideration of a broader range of issues, since individual countries and governments often place restrictions on access by, and employment of, non-nationals. Such policies can be either universal or selective. For example, within the European Union, there exists a high degree of labour mobility amongst most member states, with legislation to guarantee that citizens of the majority of EU countries are not disadvantaged when applying for jobs in countries other than that of their origin. At the same time, employment of non-EU citizens is restricted and controlled by work permits and visas granted on the basis of a consideration of the individual case. Similar restrictions apply to a greater or lesser degree across the world.

Employment of individuals from cultural backgrounds different from that of the home country not only refers to the international transfer of staff or to the recruitment of local staff in order to serve the host country market. Previously, we have mentioned the offshoring of service jobs from the UK to India, whereby Indian staff members are employed in their own country to deliver services across geographic distance and time zones to customers in the UK. Since the 1990s, the Indian call-centre industry has grown to become a major provider of services not only to the UK market, but also to the USA and Australia, with the Indian government predicting up to 1 million call-centre jobs by 2009. The recruitment and training practices involved in the employment of this staff provide a telling example of contemporary HRM within an international context (see Das and Dharwadkar, 2006). In the industry, employees are expected not only to speak English, but also to adopt elements of cultural identity associated with the country in which their tele-clients are located. The objective of this is to give the impression that the service worker is geographically in close proximity to the caller. In addition, whilst the call-centre business may operate as an outsourced contractor to multiple businesses, workers are expected to pretend that they are employed directly by the main client organization for each call answered.

As far as specific HR practices are concerned, employees are required to work anti-social hours that coincide with the day-time for the client and to take holidays at the same times as them. Moreover, they undergo intensive language training to reduce their 'mother tongue influence' (MTI) and to adopt a suitable 'local' accent. This involves, amongst other training sessions, one on critique and mockery of 'Indianism' – the particular way in which English is spoken in India – along with encouragement to support others in abandoning the Indian influence in their own speech. Workers are also indoctrinated in order to be able to reproduce socio-cultural indicators that reinforce their 'locality', such as being able to engage in casual conversation about the weather, sport and television. Additionally, following a 'naming ceremony' (Sitt, 1997), operators may adopt an appropriately English-sounding name. The requirement to conceal one's actual identity is presented to the workers as an advantage, since pretending to be someone else is supposed to make it easier for the call-centre workers to cope with the abuse they frequently endure in contact with customers.

From the company's point of view, creating the impression of geographic and cultural proximity between the service provider and the customer serves two main purposes. First, it is considered to promote higher levels of customer satisfaction and, second, it reduces the risk of any hostile reaction to the perceived loss of jobs in the client's home country. Whilst the logic behind these objectives may align with the corporate perspective and the goal of profit-maximization, enactment of the processes involved is problematic. In brief, as we have outlined above, it requires that employees, as part of their everyday job, have to lie to the customer who, in turn, is routinely deceived if the service delivery is 'successfully' performed. However, the lie is not limited to the speech act during the period when the employee is at work, but in many cases staff are actively encouraged to internalize it, such that it becomes part of their everyday life. All this happens in the spirit of acknowledging the actual cultural differences between the company's employees and customers, and 'managing' them to the organization's benefit.

international labour relations

Within a lot of IB literature, the starting point for discussion of labour relations tends to frame it as an intra- and inter-organizational process for MNEs. First, there is consideration of the nature of the firm itself, whether it is highly centralized or largely decentralized, and the extent to which it relies on codified control and reporting structures or is more informal in nature. Beyond this, there is discussion of the relationship between firms and organized labour unions, whether, like the European model, negotiations tend to take place at an industry level or, as in the USA, they occur predominantly between individual companies and the involved unions. In addition, the concept of 'industrial democracy', that is the extent to which organized labour has a legally defined role in determining employment conditions, such as wage levels, working conditions and redundancy terms, in consultation with the company management, is considered. Beyond these organizational aspects of labour relations, we can identify issues that are of concern at a global level, even though they do not enter the discourse of international industrial relations in mainstream textbooks, yet are well represented in critical texts and other media. Here, we refer to contemporary relationships of global production and consumption that exclude the possibility of organized action by groups of workers and, at the same time, do not necessitate the taking of responsibility by MNEs for the workforce that is employed in making the goods and providing the services that they sell in international markets.

As we outlined in Chapter 2, the charity War on Want has drawn attention to the working conditions of those involved in low-cost fashion garment production in Bangladesh for UK-based MNEs. It points out that these workers typically work long hours, often in unsafe conditions, are paid below the level of basic subsistence, and are denied overtime, holiday and maternity payments. At the same time, their bargaining power in relation to the employers is very low since they are also refused the right of free association and formation of an organized labour union. These conditions are in direct contravention of the conventions and recommendations of the International Labour Organization (ILO) (see Chapter 4), under the auspices of the United Nations. As War on Want (2006) highlights, the MNEs whose products are manufactured under these conditions do not have any direct responsibility for either the employment contract between their sub-contractor factory owners and the workforce, or for the working conditions and issues of health and safety. Whilst the companies identified by War on Want have all signed up to the voluntary code of conduct established under the Ethical Trading Initiative, the report cites numerous examples of breaches of the code. It also highlights the lengths to which the local contractors will go in order to influence the outcomes of social audits and to present a positive image of the working environment in their premises.

the global impact of the new labour market

The fact that, driven by the motives of profit-maximization and shareholder return, companies engaged in international business constantly seek to lower their costs – including the costs of their human resources – has important implications for social change at a global level. For example, one way of reducing expenses related to the employment of staff is by moving away from permanent and secure employment contracts, or paying employer contributions to pension funds and the healthcare insurance of the workers. Whilst, for example, in various countries within the European Union, the extent to which such practices are possible is limited by legislation, this certainly is not the case across the world. In many economies, particularly in the largely unregulated export processing zones (EPZs), workers have no rights to labour union representation, overtime payments, holiday pay, maternity leave, or any other benefits. In addition to being subjected to economic impoverishment, workers in many global industries face serious health risks on a daily basis, from the pesticides to which labourers on flower farms (e.g. in Columbia and Kenya) are exposed, to the poisonous fumes emitted by the burning of British waste exported to China.

Due to differences in national regulatory frameworks relating to employment conditions, MNEs are able to seek out the most advantageous locations for their operations – from the point of view of the cost to the company. From the perspective of the societies involved, on the other hand, these kinds of employment practices exclude citizens from developing secure and sustainable livelihoods. Additionally, as mentioned earlier in this chapter, in relation to the procurement of products and services, MNEs are often able to transfer their business between countries. At the same time, they are not obliged to address the consequences of their withdrawal from a given location, such as unemployment for the workers and the resultant impact on their families under conditions of absence of state welfare provision.

A common response to the problems highlighted above is that firms are not obliged to look after the societies they are present within, beyond ensuring that their operations do not breach the law. In line with the same logic of argument, individuals managing organizations are not seen as being responsible for the prosperity and well-being of their employees, but only for their own and that of their families. This logic is used to legitimize the unequal pay distribution in the global labour market, whereby, at present, the ratio of a CEO's pay to that of a worker is around 500:1 (Steger, 2003). The problem we see with this model of redistribution of a company's profits is that for the majority of workers – and hence for large sections of society – it becomes impossible to overcome long-term poverty or to benefit from the same life opportunities as those open to the wealthy few, both in developing and developed economies.

conclusion

In this short chapter, we have addressed the main topics relating to managing people faced by organizations involved in the field of IB and, more specifically, the implications of these for workers across the globe. The three main areas that we have focused on are culture, staffing and HRM, and labour relations. We have deliberately pointed to those aspects of these three domains that are typically not discussed in the mainstream IB texts. In relation to culture, we looked at critiques of Hofstede's approach to national cultural differences. With regard to employment policies and HR practices, we have drawn upon the example of Indian call centres in order to discuss contemporary issues of the use of international labour in their home countries in order to serve the domestic markets of MNEs. Finally, we have provided examples of international labour relations within global supply chains that lie outside the canon of the mainstream organization/labour union relationship discourse. In selecting and presenting these illustrations, we have attempted to broaden the scope of the discussion of the management of people in the IB context, and to draw your attention to issues of broad social significance at a global level.

Concluding Remarks

Everywhere do I perceive a certain conspiracy of rich men seeking their own advantage under the name and pretext of the commonwealth.

Sir Thomas More

In this short book, we have sought to provide an overview of the field of international business (IB). We have pointed to key assumptions that underpin contemporary IB, for example, that it is largely beneficial, that its growth and development is desirable, and that the generation of maximum shareholder return from it is a proper aim. In considering how we all affect or are affected by IB activities, we have reflected upon the situation of a range of parties, not only the managers of companies involved in IB activities, but also the employees, suppliers, broader society and the natural environment.

In our discussion, we have included some of the less glamorous and less widely debated forms of international business, such as ship breaking and trade in waste, along with practices such as tax avoidance. As we come towards the end of the project, we have to set out some of its limitations. In outlining the field of IB across the contexts of time, space and the disciplinary fields of theory and practice, we have obviously had to make choices about what to include and what to exclude. As such, we do not pretend that we offer a comprehensive account of IB, either with regard to the theories pertaining to the discipline or in relation to representations of IB practice. We hope, however, that we have provided pointers to further reading on theoretical domains that might offer alternative interpretations of IB activity, and have encouraged you to think more widely about what constitutes international business.

We have attempted to convince you that it is important that we all reflect upon how our thinking and acting as participants in IB affects others, the nature of the world and the possible outcomes for future generations. We hope that we have shown that the way things are now is not the only way things can be, and that there are options for a range of different futures. Primarily, we hope that we have made you think about how you can make a difference.

what we have done

In offering an overview of the field of international business, we have considered it necessary to provide an historical grounding, to show how what is taken for granted and presented as normal day-to-day IB activity in mainstream texts is based upon centuries of perpetuation and development of practices that have their origins in European colonialism. This involved, in addition to the accumulation of wealth by the colonizers, the suppression of indigenous populations in other territories and the appropriation and exploitation of the natural resources of their lands. We trust that we have succeeded in showing that we cannot separate the present from the past and view IB as ahistorical and non-contextual, as a value-free activity of a purely economic nature, and as devoid of social and environmental impacts at a global level. Having pointed to European nation states as the early key actors that set the 'rules of the game', we have argued that they established the basic principles that laid the ground for the emergence and dominance of the global (western) MNE as the major contemporary power-broker of international business. In this context, we call for a widening of participation in the debate in relation to the possibilities for alternative structures and forms of IB.

Within the confines of this text, we have sought to offer a range of perspectives that take account of the different actors involved in and affected by IB. In discussing examples of extant IB practices, we have drawn attention to the ephemeral nature of employment and income, the poor working conditions for many across the world, and the growth of socio-economic fragmentation and stratification at a global level. Whilst we have not suggested that there is one 'right' way of conducting IB in answer to current problems, we aim to stimulate your thinking on the issues that we raise, and to provoke critical reflection on your own position within IB both now and in the future.

how have we approached international business?

In order to engage critically with the nature of contemporary IB, it is necessary to consider it as a network of power relations. Contemplating the role of power, we see that, in many cases, IB activity is not based upon a free exchange, but upon very clear relationships of superior and subordinate. Our thinking on the nature and role of power leads us to a contemplation of the outcomes of IB activity: whom does it benefit and whom does it disadvantage? Who decides what is 'good' about IB, and according to whose definition of good is this determined?

Seeking a philosophical foundation for our thinking on the good and bad of IB, we challenge the dominant neo-liberal ethic by reference to the Aristotelian concept of *phronēsis*, and the question of what is 'good for man', that is for humanity in general? We find a framework for this through a contemporary interpretation of *phronēsis* in Flyvbjerg's (2001) four value-rational questions:

- Where are we going?
- Is this development desirable?
- What, if anything, should we do about it?
- Who gains and who loses, and by which mechanisms of power?

In reflecting upon Flyvbjerg's questions, we address the impact of supranational institutions that set the context for IB, such as the IMF, the World Bank and the WTO, questioning whether they act in the interests of broad civic society or are driven by those of a narrow section of the market.

At this point, we have to acknowledge that, in commenting on the power dynamics of mainstream approaches to IB, we cannot deny our own influence on your thinking, and the power that we, as authors, exercise in relation to your interpretation of the issues that we write about. Please be aware of this as you form your own view of IB as a theoretical discipline and a domain of practice. In closing, we posit one final question, one that seeks to evoke a personal answer in you, our reader, informed by your own values, beliefs, hopes and aspirations.

why does this matter to you?

As we have outlined, IB is not a value-free activity that is devoid of social, economic and environmental impacts. Neither is it an activity that is conducted by 'others' and to which we are external bystanders. We all affect the nature and impact of international business and are affected by it on a daily basis, as consumers, employees and as citizens of the world. Hence, we all have a responsibility to think about our own contributions to issues such as sweatshop labour, tax avoidance, pollution and environmental degradation.

We argue that students of IB, and those who are and who aspire to be managers, must look beyond the surface of representations of IB as a field of practice, to consider the values and beliefs of those who perpetuate it and who are the major beneficiaries of it. In exploring the underlying and often unstated assumptions about the purpose of IB, we might refer to Flyvbjerg's final question: 'Who wins and who loses, and by which mechanisms of power?' We also need to reflect critically upon what we do, how and why we do it, and what impact our actions have, or may have in the future, both locally and globally. The answer will depend upon our own values, beliefs, expectations and aspirations.

So, why *does* this matter to you?

References

Adam, D. (2006) 'Royal Society tells Exxon: stop funding climate change denial', *The Guardian*, 20 September, available at: http://www.commondreams.org/headlines06/0920-04.htm, accessed 27 January 2008.

Allianz (2007) 'Alternative finance', *Allianz Knowledge Partnersite*, available at: http://knowledge.allianz.com/en/globalissues/microfinance/alternative_finance/, accessed 18 January 2008.

Amnesty International (2003) '"Our brothers who help kill us" – economic exploitation and human rights abuses in the east', *Amnesty International Reports*, AFR 62/010/2003.

Andersen, A.B. (2001) *Worker Safety in the Ship-Breaking Industries*. Geneva: International Labour Office.

Aristotle (350BC/2004) *The Nicomachean Ethics*. Trans J.A.K. Thomson, 1953. Rev. H. Tredennick, 1976. London: Penguin Books.

Arrighi, G., Silver, B.J. and Brewer, B.C. (2003) 'Industrial convergence, globalization, and the persistence of the north–south divide', *Studies in Comparative International Development*, 38 (1): 3–31.

Balassa, P. (1962) *The Theory of Economic Integration*. London: Allen and Unwin.

Bales, K. (2000) *New Slavery*. Santa Barbara, CA: ABC–CLIO.

Baran, P.A. (1957) *The Political Economy of Growth*. New York: Monthly Review Press.

Bauman, Z. (1998) *Globalization: The human consequences*. Cambridge: Polity Press.

BBC (1999) 'In pictures: the WTO Seattle protest', *BBC News*, 1 December, available at: http://news.bbc.co.uk/1/hi/world/americas/544786.stm, accessed 18 January 2008.

BBC (2004) 'Bechtel gets new $1.8bn Iraq deal', *BBC News*, 7 January, available at: http://news.bbc.co.uk/1/hi/business/3375383.stm, accessed 18 September 2007.

BBC (2006) 'Norwich Union boss backs job cuts', *BBC News*, 14 September, available at: http://news.bbc.co.uk/1/hi/business/5345216.stm, accessed 12 September 2007.

Bello, W. (2003) *Deglobalization: Ideas for a new world economy*. London: Zed Books.

Bretton Woods Project (2005) *What are the Bretton Woods Institutions?*, available at: http://www.brettonwoodsproject.org/item.shtml?x=320747, accessed 27 January 2008.

Bukharin, N. (1917/1987) *Imperialism and the World Economy*. London: Merlin.

Cairns, G. and Śliwa, M. (2008) 'The implications of Aristotle's *phronēsis* for organizational inquiry', in D. Barry and H. Hansen (eds), *The Sage Handbook of New Approaches to Organization Studies*. London: Sage, pp. 318–31.

Cardoso, F.H. (1972) 'Dependency and development in Latin America', *New Left Review*, 74: 83–95.

Carnall, D. (1996) 'Tobacco funding for academics', *British Medical Journal*, 312: 721–2.

Conachy, J. (2004) 'Private military companies in Iraq: profiting from colonialism', *World Socialist Web Site*, 3 May, available at: http://www.wsws.org/articles/2004/may2004/pmcs-m03.shtml, accessed 13 August 2007.

Corporate Watch (2002) 'BAE Systems: a corporate profile', *Corporate Crimes*, Corporate Watch UK, 22 June, available at: http://www.corporatewatch.org.uk/?lid=184, accessed 14 August 2007.

Czinkota, M.R., Ronkainen, I.A. and Moffett, M.H. (2005) *International Business* (7th edn). Mason, OH: South-Western.

Daniels, J.D., Radebaugh, L.H. and Sullivan, D.P. (2007) *International Business: Environment and operations*. Upper Saddle River, NJ: Pearson/Prentice-Hall.

Das, D. and Dharwadkar, R. (2006) 'Cultural mimicry and hybridity: on the work of identity in international call centers in India', paper presented at the Academy of Management Conference, August, Atlanta.

Dunne, J. (1993) *Back to the Rough Ground: Practical judgment and the lure of technique*. Notre Dame, IN: University of Notre Dame Press.

Dunning, J. (1977) 'Trade, location of economic activity and the NINE: a search for an eclectic approach', in B. Ohlin, P.O. Hesselborn and P.M. Wijkman (eds), *The International Allocation of Economic Activity*. London: Macmillan, pp. 395–431.

Dunning, J. (1980) 'Toward an eclectic theory of international production: some empirical tests', *Journal of International Business Studies*, 11 (1): 9–31.

Dunning, J. (1993) *The Globalization of Business*. London: Routledge.

Dunning, J. (2000) 'The eclectic paradigm as an envelope for economic and business theories of MNE activity', *International Business Review*, 9: 163–90.

Economist (2007) 'Moving pieces: global companies have plenty of latitude to minimise their tax bills', *Economist.com Research Survey Tools*, 22 February, available at: http://www.economist.com/special-reports/displaystory.cfm?story_id=8695175, accessed 17 April 2007.

Eun, C. and Resnick, B. (2006) *International Financial Management.* London: McGraw-Hill/Irwin.

Fainaru, S. (2007) 'Iraq contractors face growing parallel war: as security work increases, so do casualties', *Washington Post Foreign Service,* 16 June, available at: http://www.washingtonpost.com/wp-dyn/content/article/2007/06/15/AR2007061502602.html?nav=emailpage, accessed 14 August 2007.

Fainaru, S. and Klein, A. (2007) 'In Iraq, a private realm of intelligence-gathering: firm extends U.S. Government's reach', *Washington Post Foreign Service,* 1 July, available at: http://www.washingtonpost.com/wp-dyn/content/article/2007/06/30/AR2007063001075.html?nav=emailpage, accessed 14 August 2007.

Fishman, C. (2007) *The Wal-Mart Effect: How an out-of-town super-store became a superpower.* London: Penguin.

Flyvbjerg, B. (2001) *Making Social Science Matter: Why social inquiry fails and how it can succeed again.* Cambridge: Cambridge University Press.

Fortune (2007) *Fortune Global 500,* Atlanta, GA: CNN, available at: http://money.cnn.com/magazines/fortune/global500/2006/index.html, accessed 17 November 2007.

Foxwell, A. (2007a) 'Norwich Union call centre U-turn', *Financial Mail on Sunday,* 28 January, available at: http://www.thisismoney.co.uk/news/article.html?in_article_id=416860&in_page_id=1&ito=1565, accessed 18 January 2008.

Foxwell, A. (2007b) 'Norwich Union's Indian disaster', *Financial Mail,* 25 March, available at: http://www.thisismoney.co.uk/investing-and-markets/article.html?in_article_id=418740&in_page_id=3, accessed 19 January 2008.

Frank, A.G. (1978) *Dependent Accumulation and Underdevelopment.* London: Macmillan.

Freeman, R.E. (1984) *Strategic Management: A stakeholder approach.* Boston: Pitman.

Friedman, M. (1962) *Capitalism and Freedom.* Chicago: University of Chicago Press.

Friedman, M. and Friedman, R. (1980) *Free to Choose: A personal statement.* London: Secker & Warburg.

Glyn, A. (2006) *Capitalism Unleashed: Finance, globalization and welfare.* Oxford: Oxford University Press.

Goetz, S.J. and Swaminathan, H. (2006) 'Wal-Mart and country-wide poverty', *Social Science Quarterly,* 87: 211–26.

Goodchild, S. and Hodgson, M. (2006) 'Tobacco industry: smoking isn't bad for your health', *The Independent* 12 July, available at: http://www.news.independent.co.uk/world/americas/article1090210.ece, accessed 12 September 2007.

Green, D. (no date) 'The rough guide to the WTO', *CAFOD Policy Papers*, available at: http://www.rufuspollock.org/wto/cache/CAFOD_rough_guide_to_WTO.html, accessed 15 December 2007.

Greenpeace (2003) 'UK's own ghost ship found in India', *Greenpeace News*, 12 November, available at: http://www.greenpeace.org/international/news/uk-s-own-ghost-ship-in-india, accessed 7 September 2007.

Greenpeace (2006) 'Draft IMO Treaty called "shockingly inadequate" in addressing global ship scrap crisis', 16 March, available at: http://www.greenpeaceweb.org/shipbreak/, accessed 5 July 2007.

Greenpeace (2007) 'Exxon: still pumping out lies', Greenpeace UK, 18 May, available at: http://www.greenpeace.org.uk/blog/climate/exxon-still-pumping-out-lies, accessed 19 September 2007.

Guardian Unlimited (1999) 'The international arms trade to Indonesia', *Guardian Unlimited Special Reports*, 9 September, available at: http://www.guardian.co.uk/indonesia/Story/0,2763,200783,00.html, accessed 11 November 2007.

Hall, E.T. and Hall, M.R. (1990) *Understanding Cultural Differences: Germans, French and Americans*. Yarmouth: Intercultural Press.

Hardt, M. and Negri, A. (2004) *Multitude: War and democracy in the age of empire*. New York: Penguin.

Harvard Business School (2008) 'Marketing', *Faculty & Research*, available at: http://www.hbs.edu/units/marketing, accessed 27 January 2008.

Heckscher, E. (1919/1950) 'The effect of foreign trade on the distribution of income', in H. Ellis and L.A. Metzler (eds), *Readings in the Theory of International Trade*. London: Allen and Unwin, pp. 272–300.

Hell, I. (2006) 'Banks move into Islamic finance', *BBC News*, 9 June, available at: http://news.bbc.co.uk/1/hi/world/middle_east/5064058.stm, accessed 18 January 2008.

Herman, M.-O., Delen, B. and Vermaerke, P. (2002) 'Supporting the war economy in the DRC: European companies and the coltan trade', *IPIS Reports*, January.

Hill, C.W.L. (2007) *International Business: Competing in the global marketplace* (6th edn). New York: McGraw-Hill/Irwin.

Hobson, J.A. (1902/1938) *Imperialism: A study*. London: George Allen and Unwin.

Hofstede, G.H. (1984) *Culture's Consequences: International differences in work-related values*. Newbury Park, CA: Sage.

Hofstede, G.H. (1997) *Cultures and Organizations: Software of the mind*. New York: McGraw-Hill.

Hofstede, G.H. and Bond, M.H. (1988) 'Confucius and economic growth: new trends in culture's consequences', *Organization Dynamics*, 16: 4–21.

Holden, N. (2002) *Cross-cultural Management: A knowledge management perspective.* Harlow: Financial Times/Prentice Hall.

House, R.J., Hanges, P.J., Javidan, M., Dorfman, P.W. and Gupta, V. (2004) *Leadership, Culture, and Organizations: The GLOBE study of 62 societies.* Thousand Oaks, CA: Sage.

Hufbauer, G.C. (1970) 'The impact of national characteristics and technology on the commodity composition of trade in manufactured goods', in R. Vernon (ed.), *The Technology Factor in International Trade.* New York: Columbia University Press, pp. 145–231.

Hymer, S. (1960/1976) *The International Operations of National Firms: A study of direct foreign investment.* Cambridge, MA: MIT Press.

Ietto-Gillies, G. (2005) *Transnational Corporations and International Production.* Cheltenham: Edward Elgar.

ILO (no date) 'About the ILO', International Labour Organization, available at: http://www.ilo.org/global/About_the_ILO/lang--en/index. htm, accessed 19 November 2007.

IMO (2002) 'Flag state implementation', International Maritime Association, available at: http://www.imo.org/, accessed 13 August 2007.

Ingham, B. (2004) *International Economics: A European focus.* Harlow: Financial Times/Prentice Hall.

Jentoft, S. (2006) 'Beyond fisheries management: The *phronetic* dimension', *Marine Policy*, 30: 671–80.

Jevons, W.S. (1871) *The Theory of Political Economy.* London: Macmillan.

Jordan, M. (2000) 'Marketers discover black Brazil', *The Wall Street Journal*, 24 November: A11, A14.

Klein, N. (2000) *No Space/No Choice/No Jobs – No Logo.* London: Flamingo.

Kotler, P. and Levy, S.J. (1969) 'Broadening the concept of marketing', *Journal of Marketing*, 33: 10–15.

Krugman, P. (1979) 'A model of innovation, technology transfer, and the world distribution of income', *The Journal of Political Economy*, 87 (2): 253–66.

Krugman, P. (1981) 'Intraindustry specialization and the gains from trade', *Journal of Political Economy*, 89: 959–73.

Lazer, W. (1969) 'Marketing's changing social relationships', *Journal of Marketing*, 33: 3–9.

Lenin, V.I. (1902/1969) *What Is To Be Done? – Burning questions of our movement.* New York: International Publishers.

Linder, S.B. (1961) *An Essay on Trade and Transformation.* New York: John Wiley.

Lobe, J. (2003) 'Global businesses profit from Congo war, groups charge', *OneWorld US*, 28 October, available at: http://www.globalpolicy.org/socecon/tncs/2003/1028congoprofit.htm, accessed 27 January 2008.

Macartney, J. (2007) 'Three Gorges Dam is a disaster in the making, China admits', *The Times*, 27 September, available at: http://www.timesonline.co.uk/tol/news/world/article2537279.ece, accessed 25 November 2007.

McSweeney, B. (2002) 'Hofstede's model of national cultural differences and their consequences: a triumph of faith – a failure of analysis', *Human Relations*, 55: 89–118.

Magala, S. (2005) *Cross-Cultural Competence*. London: Routledge.

Markusen, J.R. (1998) 'Multinational firms, location and trade', *The World Economy*, 21: 733–56.

Marshall, A. and Marshall, M.P. (1879/1994) *The Economics of Industry*. Bristol: Thoemmes.

Marx, K. and Engels, F. (1848/2002) *The Communist Manifesto*. London: Penguin.

Matt Phillips http://news.bbc.co.uk/1/hi/world/europe/679838.stm

Menger, C. (1871/1950) *Principles of Economics*. Glencoe, IL: The Free Press.

Milanovic, B. (2005) *Worlds Apart: Measuring international and global inequality*. Princeton, NJ: Princeton University Press.

Miller, G. (2004) 'Everyday low wages: the hidden price we all pay for Wal-Mart', *Democratic Staff of the Committee on Education and the Workforce*, US House of Representatives. Washington, DC: Government Printing Office.

Milmo, C. (2007) 'The slow boats to China filled with our refuse', *The Independent*, 26 January, p. 3.

Monbiot, G. (1996) 'Hawks and doves', Mobiot.com, available at: http://www.monbiot.com/archives/1996/07/30/hawks-and-doves/, accessed 2 November 2007.

Montlake, S. (2005) 'World Bank backs Laos dam project', *BBC News*, 1 April, available at: http://news.bbc.co.uk/1/hi/world/asia-pacific/4399587.stm, accessed 9 October 2007.

Morgan, G. (2003) 'Marketing and critique: prospects and problems', in M. Alvesson and H. Willmott (eds), *Studying Management Critically*. London: Sage, pp. 111–31.

Nayyar, D. (1997) 'Globalization: the game, the players and the rules', in S.D. Gupta (ed.), *The Political Economy of Globalization*. London: Kluwer.

OECD (2004) *Principles of Corporate Governance*. Paris: OECD Publications.

Ohlin, B. (1933/1967) *Interregional and International Trade*. Cambridge, MA: Harvard University Press.

Otto, B. and Böhm, S. (2006) '"The people" and resistance against international business', *Critical Perspectives on International Business*, 2: 299–320.

Perlmutter, H.V. (1969) 'The tortuous evolution of the multinational corporation', *Columbia Journal of World Business*, Jan.–Feb.: 9–18.

Porter, M. (1985) *Competitive Advantage: Creating and sustaining superior performance*. New York: Free Press.

Porter, M. (1990) *The Competitive Advantage of Nations*. New York: Free Press.

PRB (2005) 'PRB's 2005 world population data sheet reveals persisting global inequalities in health and well-being', *2005 World Population Data Sheet*, available at: http://www.prb.org/Publications/Datasheets/2005/2005WorldPopulationDataSheet.aspx, accessed 3 November 2007.

Prebisch, R. (1971) *Change and Development – Latin America's Great Task: Report submitted to the Inter-American Development Bank*. New York: Praeger.

Rahman, A. and Ullah, T. (1999) 'Ship breaking: a background paper', paper prepared for the International Labour Organization's Sectoral Activities Programme. Dhaka.

Rapley, J. (2004) *Globalization and Inequality: Neoliberalism's downward spiral*. Boulder, CO: Lynne Rienner.

Ricardo, D. (1817) *On the Principles of Political Economy and Taxation*. London: John Murray.

Ridgeway, J. (2003) 'Corporate colonialism', *The Village Voice*, 23–29 April, available at: http://www.villagevoice.com/news/0317,mondo1,43569,6.html, accessed 13 August 2007.

Ritzer, G. (1995) *The McDonaldization of Society: An Investigation into the changing character of contemporary social life*. Los Angeles: Pine Forge Press.

Roberts, T. and Hite, A. (2000) *From Modernization to Globalization: Perspectives on development and social change*. Oxford: Blackwell.

Rugman, A. and Collinson, S. (2006) *International Business*. Harlow: Prentice Hall.

Say, J.B. (1803/2001) *A Treatise on Political Economy*. Edison, NJ: Transaction Publishers.

Sharma, S. and Kumar, S. (2003) 'The military backbone of globalisation', *Race and Class*, 44: 23–39.

Sikka, P. (2003) 'Plastic bucket: $972.98', *The Guardian*, 30 June, available at: http://guardian.co.uk/money/2003/jun/30/tax.social exclusion, accessed 7 March 2008.

Sikka, P. (2007) 'There's no accounting for accountants', *Guardian Unlimited*, 29 August, available at: http://commentisfree.guardian.co.uk/prem_sikka_/2007/08/no_accounting_for_accounting_s.html, accessed 23 November 2007.

Simms, A. (2007) *Tescopoly: How one shop came out on top and why it matters*. London: Constable.

Sitt, G. (1997) *Diverted to Delhi*. New York: Filmmakers Library.

Smith, A. (1776/1999) *An Inquiry into the Nature and Causes of the Wealth of Nations*. London: Penguin.

Steger, M. (2003) *Globalization: A very short introduction*. Oxford: Oxford University Press.

Tax Justice Network http://www.taxjustice.net/cms/front_content.php?idcat=2

Tax Justice Network (2005) 'Tax us if you can', Tax Justice Network Briefing Paper, September. London: New Economics Foundation.

Tax Justice Network (2007) 'Identifying tax havens and offshore finance centres', Tax Justice Network Briefing Paper, available at: http://www.taxjustice.net/cms/upload/pdf/Identifying_Tax_Havens_Jul_07.pdf, accessed 28 January 2008.

Taylor, P. and Bain, P. (2005) 'India calling to the far away towns', *Work, Employment and Society*, 19: 261–82.

Tipton, F.B. (2008) '"Thumbs-up is a rude gesture in Australia": the presentation of culture in international business textbooks', *Critical Perspectives on International Business*, 4 (1): 7–24.

Torrens, R. (1815) *Essay on the External Corn Trade*. London: J. Hatchard.

Trouiller, P., Olliaro, P., Torreele, E., Orbinski, J., Laing, R. and Ford, N. (2002) 'Drug development for neglected diseases: a deficient market and a public-health policy failure', *The Lancet*, 360, 21 September: 885.

University of Wisconsin System (2004) 'Wal-Mart corporate record', *UW System Trust Funds*, available at: http://www.uwsa.edu/tfunds/walmart1204a.htm, accessed 28 January 2008.

Veblen, T. (1899/1995) *The Theory of the Leisure Class*. London: Penguin.

Vernon, R. (1966) 'International investment and international trade in the product life cycle', *Quarterly Journal of Economics*, 80 (2): 190–207.

Vidal, J. (2007) 'CO_2 output from shipping twice as much as airlines', *The Guardian*, 3 March, available at: http://www.guardian.co.uk/environment/2007/mar/03/travelsenvironmentalimpact.transportintheuk, accessed 25 November 2007.

Waldkirch, A. (2003) 'Vertical FDI? A host country perspective', Department of Economics Working Papers, Oregon State University, Corvallis, OR.

Wallerstein, I. (1974) *The Modern World-System*. New York: Academic Press.

Wallerstein, I. (2004) *World-Systems Analysis: An introduction*. Durham, NC: Duke University Press.

Wal-Mart (2006) *2006 Annual Report: Building smiles*. Bentonville, AR: Wal-Mart Stores, Inc.

Wal-Mart Watch (2005) 'Low prices at what cost', *Wal-Mart Watch Annual Report*. Washington, DC: Center for Community & Corporate Ethics.

Walras, L. (1874) *Éléments D'économie Politique Pure, ou théorie de la richesse sociale* (*Elements of Pure Economics, or the theory of social wealth*). Lausanne: F. Rouge.

War on Want (2006) *Fashion Victims*, War on Want, London, available at: http://www.waronwant.org/Fashion+Victims+13593.twl, accessed December 6, 2006.

War on Want (2007) 'Trade and WTO: the "free trade" threat', *Fighting Global Poverty*, available at: http://www.waronwant.org/?lid=11090, accessed 23 October 2007.

West, D. (1996) 'Countertrade: an innovative approach to marketing', *Barter News*, 36, available at: http://www.barternews.com/approach_marketing.htm, accessed 17 September 2007.

World Bank (1989) 'Articles of agreement', *About Us*, available at: http://web.worldbank.org/WBSITE/EXTERNAL/EXTABOUTUS/0,,contentMDK:20049563~pagePK:43912~menuPK:58863~piPK:36602,00.html#11, accessed 7 Novemeber 2007.

World Bank (2007) 'About us', The World Bank, available at: http://web.worldbank.org/WBSITE/EXTERNAL/EXTABOU-TUS/0,,pagePK:50004410~piPK:36602~theSitePK:29708,00.html, accessed 30 March 2007.

World Health Organization (2006) *The International Code of Marketing of Breast-milk Substitutes: Frequently asked questions*. Geneva: World Health Organization.

Wrigley, C. (2000) *BAE Systems Alternative Report 2000*. London: Campaign Against Arms Trade (CAAT).

Yamey, G. (2001) 'World Bank funds private hospital in India', *BMJ News*, 3 February, available at: http://www.bmj.com/cgi/content/full/322/7281/257/a, accessed 3 December 2007.

Index